rose

rose

love in violent times

inga muscio

Seven Stories Press

NEW YORK

Seven Stories Press
140 Watts Street
New York, NY 10013
www.sevenstories.com

In Canada: Publishers Group Canada, 559 College Street, Suite 402, Toronto, ON M6G 1A9

In the UK: Turnaround Publisher Services Ltd., Unit 3, Olympia Trading Estate, Coburg Road, Wood Green, London N22 6TZ

In Australia: Palgrave Macmillan, 15-19 Claremont Street, South Yarra, VIC 3141

College professors may order examination copies of Seven Stories Press titles for a free six-month trial period. To order, visit http://www.sevenstories.com/textbook or send a fax on school letterhead to (212) 226-1411.

Book design by Jon Gilbert

Library of Congress Cataloging-in-Publication Data

Muscio, Inga.
  Rose : love in violent times / Inga Muscio. -- Seven Stories Press 1st ed.
    p. cm.
  ISBN 978-1-58322-926-2 (pbk.)
  1. Violence--Social aspects. 2. Love. I. Title.
  HM1116.M87 2010
  179.7--dc22
                                      2010039366

Printed in the United States

9 8 7 6 5 4 3 2 1

This is dedicated to my brother, Nick.
Your love lives on.

And also to Misty Tenderlove,
for protecting my solitude.

It's such a good feeling to know you're alive.
It's such a happy feeling: You're growing inside.
And when you wake up ready to say,
"I think I'll make a snappy new day."

—FRED ROGERS

Contents

Introduction

The other day I was outside my home, tearing up pieces of bread for the neighborhood crows.

You know, a regular ol' anyday afternoon.

An elderly woman I'd never seen before approached me at quite a clip.

"What are you doing?" she asked.

It was one of those annoying questions where the answer is unimportant, for the question is, in fact, an opening salvo for some other item on the agenda.

"I am feeding the birds," I responded, awaiting with bated breath the news of her actual concern.

"Oh, well, the crows are going to eat it, you know."

"Yes, the crows are highly intelligent, and they know I come out around this time every day to feed them."

"You *feed* the crows? Why *ever* would you feed the crows?"

"Because they're members of the community. I feed the other birds closer to my house, where the crows aren't comfortable landing."

"I hate the crows," she said with rattlesnake venom. "They land on my golf cart and get into my lunch. They even open packages of my food! I can't understand why you'd feed them!"

I gave the crows a silent shout-out and wondered if they figured out how to unlatch her cooler.

"Well, we're different then. If you bring extra food for the crows when you golf, perhaps they will stay out of your lunch. You can get day-old bread at very reasonable prices from any bakery outlet store."

The idea visibly repulsed her. "Humph! No one on the golf course would appreciate *that*," she said and marched off in a huff.

I hollered after her, "The crows would appreciate it!"

Most folks would probably not consider this a violent encounter. And yet, the lady intruded upon my quiet bread-breaking meditation and trampled on a moment of my life.

I have learned to pay attention to the way such interactions make me feel. This one left me feeling shitty, like the pall that falls over a party when an obnoxious drunk shows up. Her hatred of the crows resonated into the little world we shared. I felt it very strongly, as was her intention.

According to the *Oxford American Dictionary*, violence is:

- behavior involving physical force intended to hurt, damage, or kill someone or something

- strength of emotion or an unpleasant or destructive natural force: *the violence of her own feelings*

- the unlawful exercise of physical force or intimidation by the exhibition of such force

This definition does a good job of defining certain, well-touted aspects of violence, but it does not define violence.

According to this definition, former BP CEO Tony Hayward did not commit violence when he calmly admitted that he didn't prepare for a drill-baby-drill disaster and instead complained, "I'd like my life back." According to the *Oxford American Dictionary*, the influential right-wing think tank the Heritage Foundation does not commit violence when it proclaims that sex crimes against children are too harshly punished.

If we were to understand, *truly* understand, violence and the (often sacred) place it has in the world, and then took that historical imperative into the present and observed how we perpetuate violence as a matter of course in our daily lives, if we learned to see the violence surrounding us, then maybe we could learn to love.

And I mean truly love.

It is difficult to love when you live in a culture of violence.

We live in a culture of violence.

Almost all of our violence is rooted in religion and war.

Many people are raised to believe in religion and war.

I was raised to believe in dictionaries, the ocean, and my mother's roses—in the sanctity and power of life and words.

Lotsa people believe in life and words, but none of them command power in the halls of commerce, in the government, or the military—that is, the folks featured in the present power dynamic that destroys life.

It's a long shot, but perhaps if we can change ourselves, we can change the present power dynamic.

Here in the US, when, exactly, did/will slavery and the genocide of indians end? How about the occupations of Vietnam, Iraq, and Afghanistan?

Or the many ecocides taking place so men can make money?

Where do you think acts of great violence *go* once they've occurred? Do they fall off the planet, never to be seen or heard from again?

Violence does not exist in a vacuum—it has concentric properties. Like screams into the Grand Canyon, acts of violence echo back so many times it is impossible to discern the precise point at which they end.

Repercussions of all of this great violence live on in our everyday lives.

I know people adore taking solace in thinking that we are at the mercy of things much bigger and meaner than us—amorphous monsters and conspiracies that destroy the world, rape children, snuff jobs, foreclose homes, cause drug problems, and make life generally stressful, if not unbearable.

We are, however, unwilling to hold ourselves accountable for any of this.

Make no mistake—most forces of violence *are* bigger than any individual. Yet, they also live in our most intimate lives, inform our own choices and relationships. If we want to have a better world, we cannot shy away from these complexities.

Two short decades ago in the US, children did not fear going outside to play.

Playing outside all hours of the day and night was *normal* when I was a kid. There were at least twenty-five kids who played big outside games together on our block. Different blocks had different kid packs. We'd play for six hours straight on some summer nights, and the only reason a parent showed up was to tell somebody it was time for dinner or to get on home. Often it wasn't even a parent, but a deeply peeved teenage sibling who had *much* better things to do.

And don't talk about play dates being "in" now. Play dates are contrived, anemic replacements for the rollicking spontaneity of kid packs playing big games on the block.

I hardly ever see kids playing outside, and when I do, there's usually a parent nearby. It is heartbreaking. Parents have to *check in.* They have to worry and fret on *some level,* maybe just a low hum of awareness. Parents know their kids are probably 97% safe, but no one's taking that 3% for granted, either.

These days, we are all aware of violence and very much afraid. Gun ownership is considered pretty much de rigueur at this point.

It would benefit us all to better understand what we are so afraid of.

And that, in fact, we *are* afraid. Our fears are evidenced by rote daily actions—ones we do not think about one way or another: locking doors and windows, not parking in dark spots alone, teaching the kids to say, "My mom is busy right now," instead of, "Oh, she's not here, can I take a message?" Car alarms, security systems, bars on the windows, body guards—positively scads of fully everyday behaviors and realities are rooted in the fear of violence.

How does this shape our population?

The teachings and legacy of Mahatma Gandhi offer up a more comprehensive understanding of violence than *Oxford American.*

C'mon, now.

Mahatma Gandhi witnessed many crimes against humanity and the earth. Gandhi was not just a student of peace and love and other nice things like that. He was victimized and bore direct witness to mass crimes carried out by the British and their Indian minions.

He was a grim observer of violence.

Clearly and holistically, with compassion and understanding, Mahatma Gandhi apprehended violence.

The teaching in which Gandhi best defined violence for me is conveyed by his grandson Arun in the foreword to a book called *Nonviolent Communication: A Language of Life* by Marshall B. Rosenberg.

Arun Gandhi tells of the time he endured a lot of racist violence while living in South Africa with his immediate family. The black kids kicked his ass, and the white kids kicked his ass too. Fearing that he would become a bitter, resentful, violent person, his parents thought Grandpa might set him on a good path, so they took him to stay in India for a time.

"We don't often acknowledge our violence because we are ignorant about it," Arun writes. "We assume we are not violent because our vision of violence is one of fighting, killing, beating and wars—the type of things average individuals don't do."

Mahatma Gandhi wanted his thirteen-year-old grandson to truly understand nonviolence. In order to do this, Arun first needed to apprehend the true nature of violence, in all its manifestations:

> To bring this home to me, grandfather had me draw a family tree of violence using the same principles as are used for a genealogical tree. His argument was that I would have a better appreciation of nonviolence if I understood and acknowledged the violence that exists in the world. He assisted me every evening to analyze the day's happenings—everything that I experienced, read about, saw or did to others—and put them down on the tree either under "physical" (if it was violence where physical force was used) or under "passive" (if it was the type of violence where the hurt was more emotional).
>
> Within a few months I covered one wall in my room with acts of "passive" violence that grandfather described as being more insidious than "physical" violence. *He then explained that passive violence ultimately generated anger in the victim who, as an individual or as a member of a collective, responded violently. In other words, it is passive violence that fuels the fire of physical violence.* It is because we don't understand or appreciate this concept that all our efforts to work for peace have either not fructified, or the peace we achieved was only temporary. How can we extinguish a fire if we don't first cut off the fuel that ignites the inferno?

Nonviolent Communication left a lot to be desired for me. It talks about how people can respond to passively violent situations by describing what they have heard the other person saying. I can always tell when someone has read this book. They say stuff like, "I hear you saying I am full of shit. How might I appear less full of shit for you?"

And I'll say stuff like, "Well, you could stop talking to me, looking at me, and interacting with me in any capacity. That would be an awesome start."

The book does contain some interesting ideas about how we communicate with one another, but it was, all told, Arun Gandhi's foreword that slid into my consciousness like molten lava, enflaming my synapses into figuring this shit out.

"This shit" being the definition of violence.

Suddenly I saw an entire realm of violence I had never recognized *as violence* before.

I was like, "Fucken' ayyy! This is some violent shit I live in here."

By incorporating passive violence into my understanding, I clearly saw the *continuum* of violence that marshals forth this environment/culture as well as the multigenerational indoctrination required to sustain it. I understood that in order to truly love, to heal, and to make a positive contribution to the world, I had to bear witness to all the types of violence around me and find ways not to generate more of it myself.

I've thought of a list of acts of passive violence. Please note that many of these violent acts are incredibly mundane and yet often carry over into physical violence of some kind.

Betrayal

Sabotage

Creating hierarchies

Lying

Cheating

Stealing

Racism

Homophobia

Infidelity (a form of lying)

Sexism

Gossip

Shunning

Passive aggression

Mean-spirited, unnecessary litigation

Mean-spirited, unnecessary anything, really

Stalking

Bullying

Scapegoating

Emotional, psychological, and/or verbal abuse

Sex abuse grooming, of children and adults

Hijacking dreams

Social humiliation/rejection

Drug abuse/alcoholism

Fill-in-the-blank rage: road rage, chat rage, parking lot rage, etc.

Low-level, simmering rage

Ignoring/silent treatment

I conjured that list up pretty much off the top of my head. The good lordisa knows it's incomplete.

Reality show producers rely on that list, and the passive violence often escalates into physical violence on national teevee, and the ratings, oh, the ratings soar. The gossip media showcases many of these acts of violence; more and more people consider it acceptable to treat each other like total shit. Our self-worth is so invested in what we've "accomplished" and the things we own that we are liable to hurt ourselves and the people we love when we lose a job or don't measure up in some other way.

Westerners marvel at the deep sense of honor that Japanese businesspeople instill in their careers without recognizing that we have our own version of a cold-bloodedly cutthroat social system too.

Doctors, lawyers, CEOs, and various celebrities are valued. Unless they lose everything. Then they—quite rationally, given the cultural milieu—see themselves as valueless. This is when "successful" people are given to suicide.

If you lose your "value," resorting to violence can easily happen, especially if you're a white man with a bloated sense of entitlement.

Violence against women is a global pandemic, and in the US violence toward women in the media has increased 120 percent since 2004, when George Bush's reign lowered the bar in our collective consciousness.

Artists are not valued. Nor are teachers, small farmers, small business owners, or librarians.

These folks—especially artists—commit suicide all the fucken time.

And yet, some violence sustains life.

The wisdom tooth that must go—oh, that is a violent affair.

Birth is violent. The poor infant is forcefully expelled from all it knows of safety and warmth. Still, it must happen. Once you're in there, there's no getting around having to come out.

The wind is relentlessly violent and *nothing* can stop it. The Santa Ana winds, which seasonally torment the area where I grew up, even inspire violence in people and cause an influx of trauma and domestic violence patients to the emergency room. My mom worked in the hospital. A week or so into the Santa Ana winds, she'd come home from work late, exhausted, blood on her uniform, and a haunted light in her eyes.

She dreaded the Santa Ana winds. As did, according to her, the town's police, fire folks, and ambulance drivers.

In Arles, France, they have hot winds too, and that is where Vincent Van Gogh lived when he cut his ear off.

The carrot from my garden suffers greatly when I pull it from the ground. And—depending on how thinly I slice it—Mr. Carrot experiences quite a torturous death to become part of my salad.

Speaking of salads, I recently spent six hours uprooting folks from their homes to make way for my vegetables, greens, and jasmine. I was no different from a member of any occupying force, yanking out unwanted dandelion and turf, tearing roly-polys and earthworms from their quiet little homes. Later, if necessary, I will set death traps for slugs and schedule murderous aphid patrols. I will seek out and kill their utterly defenseless babies without batting an eyelash. In the name of the plant lives I ordain to exist, many must die.

Gardening is some violent-assed shit.

The procurement of meat is pretty violent.

I understand that eating meat is a way to sustain life for many populations, and this is willful death just like the carrot for my hippy-assed vegetarian salad. It is murder, and it must occur.

Just as violence is inadequately defined in our dictionaries, so too is love. The definition of love, as explained in the *Oxford American Dictionary*, is:

◎   an intense feeling of deep affection

◎   a deep romantic or sexual attachment to someone

That's love?

Big whoop dee twiddle dee doo.

That isn't how I experience love, and I bet if you were to sit down and think on it, that does not describe how love moves in your life either. Love is the result of deep communication, puny life–mocking power, and horrible beauty all coming together, in auspiciousness and awe, with liberty and justice for all. Love is giving up your kidney so someone can live, holding someone close when they are frightened or scared. Love is knowing everyone has failings and keeping them ever more close to your heart. Love accepts failure, your own as well as other people's. Love is making food, cleaning house, driving out a winter chill with hot cocoa, feeling absolute rapture when you give your lover an orgasm, sewing up a teddy bear or hot gluing a doll's hair back on, listening to a sordid tale and not passing judgment. Love is forking over money to a homeless person, giving your clothes to a domestic violence shelter, washing the windows for an elderly person, and walking the kids to the swimming pool. Love goes on and on and on. It is positively endless and cannot be defined in two short sentences about deep affection and romance.

For me, personally, the dictionary, the ocean, and my mother's roses are examples of this wondrous, life-giving phenomenon. And conversely, love is not always—or even often—sweet and nice and easy. This is mirrored in my deep-seated loathing of the dictionary, the terror and death the ocean can bring, and the hideousness of roses in the winter.

You might notice that my definition of love involves a lot of sharing.

Sharing time, sharing space in your heart, sharing intimacy.

Here, in the US, there's a commercial for Reese's Peanut Butter Cups. Since there are two candies per package, the possibility of sharing is quite present. In this commercial: pretty cursive writing unfurls across a blank screen:

Sharing is nice.

Then the screen goes blank again, and more pretty cursive writing unfurls. This time it says:

Stupid, but nice.

This is "just an ad." No harm meant. It's also the result of a series of meetings where people sat around and brainstormed a way to sell candy. It was decided that mean-spiritedness, greed, and selfishness appeals to the candy-buying public.

The stupidity of sharing is, at present, a value we hold dear to our Ponzi-scheming capitalist hearts. Sharing is borderline communist behavior.

Why give someone a piece of your candy when *you* could enjoy two pieces? This value is deeply entrenched in most aspects of government, commerce, and the media, and it comes from the frontier values we are indoctrinated to appreciate. Why should the indians have any land? Why allow the wolves to eat the moose and elk we wish to hunt? Why should small, organic farms take up space that could be used for agriculture conglomerates? Why not keep drilling for oil off the coastlines even after it's been proven that the ultimate cost far outweighs the potential monetary profit? Why keep that old ornate theater when it could generate more income as a parking lot? Why make friends with that poor girl from the sticks when everyone else in our dorm is from a wealthy West Coast family? Why offer royalties to musicians if the music industry is in its fledgling years and musicians honestly have no idea that there is money to be made throughout their lives?

Violence, in its many, many manifestations, is bigger than us, and there is fuckall we can do to "change" this shitassly dog-eat-dog, ecocidal, homicidal, pedophile-assed, sexually terrorizing environment/culture.

So I suppose it does, indeed, make a kind of sense to passively, unconsciously partake 'cause *you* can't make everything all right. But all this passive partaking eats us up inside, and for those who recognize this loss of humanity, there are plenty of options.

What do we know for sure we can do?

First and foremost, we can learn to love and to live with love in our hearts, every livelong day of our lives.

Love as a *lifestyle* is a series of actions and choices that take place moment by moment. Sometimes love is nice and sweet, and sometimes love means having the clarity of mind, courage, and self-worth to make firm boundaries with those who treat you—or others—poorly. The others part matters greatly in love, for there is no distinction between self and others. You inherently want others to be loved as you wish to be loved. You *want* to share your candy because sharing brings joy and that little smidge of joy echoes out into the world just like violence does.

Just as we fail to see the violence that surrounds us, we also fail to see the many forms of love that surround us.

Recently, everyone was all aflutter over a German Shepherd named Buddy who led a trooper to his family's burning rural home. Their home was not easy to locate, and without Buddy leading the way down curvy side roads, their entire home would have been lost.

Buddy's a fucking miracle dog! An incredible canine! How was the trooper able to understand Buddy?!? "I dunno, I dunno. I really don't know how it happened. I just went with my gut and trusted him." Buddy received a stainless steel food bowl and a medal for his valor.

My god, are you people *serious*?

Animals communicate with us all the time.

Slaughterhouses are noisy places because cows and pigs and chickens begging for their lives make quite a racket, but no one is willing to listen to them because it does not serve our value judgments, unconsidered beliefs, and pathological self-interests to do so.

People positively marvel over the miracle of nature or animals communicating with us, and yet the *real* miracle is that from time to time, people actually pay attention long enough to listen.

It is so dang important to us that we are more intelligent, more evolved, and well, more important than everything else that in the process we disconnect ourselves from so much love that can arise from our being present in the world. We want to feel like we're in control at all times, that the ways we have been taught are the Right Ways of Thinking, that anything the planet has to offer is unquestionably ours for the taking, and most of all, that nothing is bigger than us.

I've never been able to wrap my mind around this belief, for I had a big lesson on how small I am when I was a kid.

My father believed that children remembered water from being in the womb and would naturally swim, which is why he threw us in a swimming pool when we were just a few months old. That's how all four of us learned to swim. Our mom did not like this practice, but it was a nice controlled setting, so she went along with it. According to our dad, children who cannot swim have to go through a process of *learning* to be afraid of the water.

I like this theory, with the caveat that not all children have a good experience in their mother's body and getting out of it is just an ass-busting relief. Some mothers-to-be are in abusive environments, some deal with illness or extreme stress. Some mothers don't want to be pregnant at all. I imagine life in the womb could be deeply unsettling to a developing body and soul, and maybe water wouldn't carry positive associations from the get-go.

Our mom liked being pregnant.

She used to sing us lullabies, inviting us to stay inside of her as long as we wanted. She was terrified that once we were outside of her body, she could no longer keep us safe in the violent environment that awaited us.

Having been raped by two men at the age of nine, our mother was acutely aware of how unsafe this violent environment could be for a child.

When we were two or so, our dad tossed us into the ocean. Swimming in the pool as babies, it turned out, was just the training period for the real swimming lessons.

Despite his theory being borne out time after time, to this day our mom thinks he sucks for tossing her toddlers into the sea.

So I was born, and when I made it past two, it was ocean time.

I guess I was ready because I never feared swimming in the ocean. By the time I was five, body surfing was a perfect expression of my nature.

Having four strong swimmers was a comfort, but both of my parents remained cautious. We were told that the water could take us at any time and, if this happened, remember not to panic.

Do not panic.

Panic is death.

And even if you are little and death doesn't really mean much to you, you still want to keep being alive. Everyone—polar bear, mildew, praying mantis—will fight for their life if they can.

So it came to pass that a wave took me.

I immediately knew from the sheer force of it that it was much bigger than me and I was probably gonna die, but I did not panic. I knew if I panicked, things would go badly, fast. So I enjoyed the anarchy of being churned in the waves, and right when my lungs should have been fighting for air, I melted into the ocean.

I just gave it up to the lord and felt my body becoming part of something much, much bigger than me.

Then, right when I completely relaxed into not having any air, the ocean spat me out onto the shore, like a sodden, stuffed bunny rabbit.

Breathing air, tasting air, thinking about air, saying, "God, air is good."

The memory is and remains one of the most wonderful experiences I ever had in my life. I was *thrilled* to have the sensation of being a tiny part of this inconceivably massive body of water. I was a ribbon of life sloshing in the waves. I felt the ocean speaking into my body, washing over my cells, intoning vocabulary words from forever, and god, laughing, having the exact same fun cats have with sparkly strings.

The ocean played me until the last possible second of consciousness, and it was still laughing when it tossed me out, the same way I can envision our dad laughing when he tossed me in.

The message I got from this experience will, barring dementia, remain with me until the day I die.

Some things are bigger than me.

Know when something is bigger.

Know it well.

Besides the ocean, I've happened upon a number of bigger-and-more-powerful-than-me things.

Sex, death, the world, and the environment I was born into are all much bigger than me.

Within my environment, global finance; racism; sexism; violence of all kinds; corporations and their interests; the world's animal, vegetable, and mineral holocaust; slavery; and history are all bigger than me.

The plastic island vortex in the Pacific Ocean that is twice the size of Texas.

The freakish stupidity and manipulative behavior of the media/advertising industry.

The 70 percent of women soldiers who are sexually assaulted.

The staggering amount of children who have, are now, or will be suffering sexual abuse, disease, neglect, trafficking, and/or poverty.

All of these realities are bigger than anybody.

A lot of things that I would give my life to end are bigger than me.

But that doesn't mean we are powerless within these bigger things. When we know and respect our place within them, we actually have a lot of power.

My place in the ocean that time was completely negligible. I imagined myself a ribbon of seaweed, sloshing about. I knew my place, and I did not try to fight it. This decision saved my life, which is pretty powerful, don'tcha think?

There are many bad things happening in the world that inspire folks to—like most people in any abusive situation—treat ourselves, each other, and the world badly. The inverse is also, therefore, true. If we treat ourselves, each other, and the world with love, then good things will happen in the world.

If we learn about violence and we learn how to love, the possibilities are endless.

That's the idea of this book.

I hope it resonates.

PART I

VIOLENCE

We can't become what we need to be by remaining what we are.

—OPRAH

Chapter 1: **The Violence of War**

A frontier nation is one that was once considered to be a frontier by whites who were completely oblivious and nullifying of the people who were already living there. The US, Canada, New Zealand, Australia, Israel, and South Africa are all frontier nations. Not unlike empire-building nations of days gone by, frontier nations present their own special brand of sociopathic disconnect that other nations that came about through migration or good old fashioned gene-intermingling conquest do not seem to have. Frontier nations produce individuals with a sociopathic sense of entitlement toward the earth and everything that lives on it. In frontier nations, it makes perfect sense to bore an eight-mile hole into the earth and brutally enslave those who work in the hole in a quest for diamonds. If "successful," this quest will grotesquely enrich a relative handful of people on the planet. It makes sense to enslave. It makes sense to rape and murder those who may oppose the idea of a frontier. It makes sense to do a lot of shitty things.

And in this manner, we find a unique environment/culture and a unique indoctrination where violence is overlooked because it has "always" been so.

When things are believed to have "always" been the way they are, we are separated from the damage our violence inflicts on the world around us and on our relationships and self-esteem. We remove ourselves from the natural world and from our own humanity.

I was raised to believe that the military was an evil industry. My parents and extended family never had a good thing to say about war or the military. My father served in the Air Force, and I figured he knew what he was talking about.

People who join the armed services are idiots. The government uses soldiers like housewives use paper towels. If someone trains as a soldier and learns to kill, well, if they are killed, then tough shit. That's what you get for letting the government use you. The thought of joining the military myself never, ever, *ever* occurred to me.

My indoctrination and its subsequent value judgments impeded my ability to think clearly. I had never questioned the beliefs passed down to me. Like most people, I thought what my family taught me to think.

I was in my thirties and still very much under the influence of unconsidered opinions regarding war and the military when I met Stan Goff, an author, lecturer, community organizer, and retired Special Forces Master Sergeant in the US Army.

Stan Goff is not brainless nor idiotic, and at no point in his life did he deserve to die. To think otherwise is barbaric and insulting. He is a brilliantly sensitive genius of a man. Raised in a very poor town in Missouri, his choices, as he understood them, were to work in the factory that his father and mother worked in or join the military. College was out of the question. It was never posed as an option, just as joining the military was never an option for me. Stan did not want to spend his life in the factory, so he joined the army when he was eighteen. There he remained, into his forties. During this time, he learned a lot about our country and government, about corruption, masculinity, homophobia, racism, feminism, sexual violence, and capitalism. Read his books if you want to know what he learned.

The army was college for Stan.

He came out of it with the lived-experience equivalent of a doctorate in foreign policy, global economics, military strategy, Marxism, feminist theory, and race history in the US.

In one afternoon with Stan Goff, my indoctrination about the military was completely, lovingly, patiently shot to shit.

My family was wrong about the military. It is not filled with brainless automatons who deserve to die. It is filled with complex people making complex life decisions in complex ways and dealing with the subsequent complexities.

The value judgments and unconsidered beliefs of indoctrination miserably and always fail to regard complexities.

Life is this: filled with complexities.

Be all of this as it may, my family did not necessarily teach me wrong on war.

War is a wildly successful business venture from which a small population of wealthy people benefits enormously and a very large population of armed forces and innocent civilians suffers even more enormously. The military provides the workers that serve the business of the wealthy.

When rock stars want money, they go on tour.

When governments want money, they go to war.

Daily fear and xenophobia indoctrinations, courtesy of the mainstream media, prevent much of our population from seeing war for what it is. Up until the late 1970s, the mainstream media was a Rottweiler, always on corporate and government asses. This is how Watergate happened. Now, Watergate would never happen, no matter how many times the media attaches the suffix "gate" to some scandal or another. In the 1980s, the media got good at being the corporate government's cute lil' Pekingese, incessantly yapping at anyone who got too close. Sometime after 2001, the media became a Rottweiler again, but this time around, rabidly protecting corporate and government interests.

For example, the mainstream media teaches that we must sacrifice in war in order to protect our innocent civilians here at home. Meanwhile, not all of the items sold as war are, in fact, actual war, and none of our "innocents" are necessarily involved.

There are happenings we are indoctrinated to call "war" and there are happenings we would otherwise refer to as "brutal occupations" if our media-induced indoctrination did not impair our perception and vocabulary. The last war that the US was involved in—where two sides were fighting one another and it was in our nation's best interest (despite the hue and cry from the wealthy Bush ancestor/eugenic/white supremacist sector) to engage in warfare— was World War II.

What took place in the Philippines, Korea, Vietnam, Central America, Somalia, and presently, in Iraq and Afghanistan— though called so—were never wars. They were and/or remain brutal occupations.

In some countries, such as Laos, we simply dropped our bombs left over from routine sorties over Vietnam. Our grandfathers, dads, and uncles dropped them from the sky for no reason at all. Well, wait, there was *a reason*. The reason was to empty their cargo so they could land their planes safely and tuck into dinner and bed.

For this reason and in this way, we are still killing Laotian people *almost half a century* after brutally occupying their fucken' *neighbors*.

That's not "war," it's not even a brutal occupation. It is the serial time-lapse murder and maiming of children, farms, animals, and ecosystems for multiple generations. But we don't call it murder. We don't call it anything. The experience of Laotian people does not factor into our education or collective consciousness at all.

I know something we can call it. We can call it the loss of legs and arms in 1978, 1985, 1993, 1999, 2004, and 2010. We can call it no wheelchairs or financial reparation of any kind. We can call it perpetual collateral damage.

There is another quite crucial complexity of war that, in our indoctrinations, we fail to recognize.

There are long-term consequences.

The brutal occupation of Vietnam detrimentally affected the upbringing of millions of children throughout the world, who, in turn, grew up experiencing this violence, whether they were aware of its origins or not. The lives of Vietnamese families were shattered, many became refugees, and many children ended up being raised by the invaders. The occupation came home and lived on in the hearts of fathers, uncles, and grandfathers, who became alcoholics, drug addicts, abusers, rapists, chronically depressed PTSD sufferers, and/or altogether homeless absentees.

Their children are now parents, and it is hit-and-miss how they fare in the world.

When does the violence from the occupations of Iraq and Afghanistan end? Do you think it ends when the troops come home?

For many, that is when the violence of "war" just getsa brewing up.

In *Daughters of Copper Woman*, a telling of Nootka history, author Anne Cameron relays the belief that once a people kill others and taste the adrenaline rush of warfare, it takes four generations of peace for the *entire* population to recover. Mass bloodshed makes people crazy. In the US and some of the other frontier nations, there has *never* been a time of peace, so you gotta figure, without the benefit of some serious soul searching, we're all fucken' koo-koo for cocoa puffs by now.

As of this writing, at least 121 homicides have been committed by soldiers who are now home. I do not know how many children and adults have been raped by troops who have returned home, but rape statistics throughout the US are absolutely skyrocketing. We won't be holding steady at one out of four much longer.

I got that 121 statistic from a three-part article titled "Across America, Deadly Echoes of Foreign Battles" from January 13, 2008, in the *New York Times*, which states quite clearly that their research was in no way exhaustive:

This reporting most likely uncovered only the minimum number of such cases, given that not all killings, especially in big cities and on military bases, are reported publicly or in detail. Also, it was often not possible to determine the deployment history of other service members arrested on homicide charges.

This is the first time I have seen a mainstream news source offer a compelling investigation of the long-term effects of brutal occupations and wars. The article explains:

> Town by town across the country, headlines have been telling similar stories: "Family Blames Iraq after Son Kills Wife" (Lakewood, Washington), "Soldier Charged with Murder Testifies about Postwar Stress" (Pierre, South Dakota), "Iraq War Vets Suspected in Two Slayings, Crime Ring" (Colorado Springs).
>
> Individually, these are stories of local crimes, gut-wrenching postscripts to the war for the military men, their victims, and their communities. Taken together, they paint a patchwork picture of a quiet phenomenon, tracing a cross-country trail of death and heartbreak.

Colorado Springs must be a notedly violent place to live right now. In February 2008, three soldiers there killed another soldier at the tail end of a long night ah-drinkin'. One of these charmers has a photograph of himself in Iraq up on MySpace, holding up a dead cat. The caption, of course, says, "Killed another Iraq pussy." Another one's MySpace motto is "Chillin' and Killin'," and he sports a dramatically fetching SS tattoo on the inside of his forearm.

The *New York Times* article does not discuss any form of violence besides murder, nor does it focus on any female soldiers. It is worth mentioning that, according to a 2009 Pentagon report, one in three female soldiers will experience sexual assault while serving in the military.

Less than a month after this article came out, the AP newswire reported that a female soldier stationed in Fort Lewis, Washington, killed a couple, both of whom were also serving in the military, and kidnapped their seven-month-old baby.

Consider all of the children now being raised by men and women who might not be in the best mental state. This is what happened after the brutal occupation of Vietnam, and it's what happened after WWI and WWII.

It appears to be a cycle of violence to me.

A young person signs up, seeking community, direction, resources for higher education, leadership skills, a chance to kick some serious ass, or the right to "defend" one's country. If this young person is of color, there is a good chance military recruiters stalked them—without their parent's knowledge—plying them with pizza, video games, and promises of a better future.

You train.

You learn.

You get yelled at, humiliated, possibly abused, and you make friends.

These friends are not like other friends. You count on these friends, and they count on you. In combat, your friends are the people who make sure you stay alive or who retrieve your body so your family will have someone to bury. They are much more important than civilian friends. If you see one of these friends doing something horrifying—raping, humiliating, beating, killing—you don't tell. You keep your mouth shut and learn to deal with it. If you see limbless children laying in pools of blood, dead pregnant women, life snuffed before your very eyes again and again—well, it is painful. But you are in no position to allow yourself the luxury of feeling pain. So maybe you bottle it up and maybe *you* join in and do terrible things that you very well know would break your mother's heart.

You maybe look away while something horrible is happening to someone and your gut is clenching because you want to stop it, but you know you are completely powerless to do anything. You witness or perpetuate horrible acts of violence. You are raped or relentlessly sexually terrorized. All these things exact a huge toll on our men and women in uniform.

If not now, then in the future, for, without therapy, it will definitely show up in their children.

And you know, when a soldier comes home, wouldn't that be surreal? Everyone acting like you have not seen a child's head explode because no one else is haunted by such images, nor do they want to be, nor are they capable of hearing you deal with all the things you have seen. And even if you are blessed with sensitive, caring listeners, you probably won't be able to talk about it for a while. You need to adjust, but there is no buffer zone for you, there is no safe harbor.

So buck up, get a job, go to school, and act normal.

My god, yes.

I can see how and why soldiers might reach critical mass and set off concentric explosions of violence in their homes or communities.

Violence is not easily contained.

It lives on in intimate relationships. And see how this problem kinda compounds in a world filled with war, poverty, mass rape, starvation, disease, and dear god, what else?

I remember in the movie *Bowling for Columbine* Michael Moore went around asking people why the US was so much more violent than Canada. There are a lot of guns in Canada, and most of the same teevee shows, movies, advertisements, and video games serve to indoctrinate the population. Mr. Moore seemed to suggest that the fear mongering in the news media was largely responsible. Though this is definitely part of the phenomena, I respectfully beg to differ.

Our penchant for sending our children off to brutal occupations that politicians, businessmen, and reporters call "wars" is responsible. Our endless propagandizing about why this kind of violence is necessary is responsible. Canadians were not raised by people whose fathers raped, murdered, and pillaged Vietnamese lives and then came home with all their nightmares intact. Canadians do not teach schoolchildren that the death of one hundred thousand Japanese via the atomic bomb was "necessary." That the death of one million Iraqis was to "protect freedom." That's why the US is more violent than Canada. We validate and facilitate violence every day and have done so throughout our history.

And through all of this, it must be acknowledged that war has been happening for a long, long, long time. We can't stop war or brutal occupations from happening, but we can take a look at why great violence is a commodity within, and by-product of, our culture/environment.

One afternoon around the 2008 election, a Somali woman and I got into an election conversation.

She said, "I love George W. Bush. I will miss him."

I thought I had not heard her correctly.

She is, after all, a Muslim refugee who never benefited from the policies of the Bush administration. I have never heard a Muslim person express any goodwill toward this man. I teach English to refugees and a lot of my students are from Somalia. If George W. Bush is mentioned for some reason, a pantomime of spitting on the floor tends to occur.

I didn't have a chance to say anything before she jumped off on my body language, as so many Somali folks I know tend to do.

"You don't love George Bush, but I do, and you know why I love George Bush?"

Again, she did not wait for my reply.

She knew I wanted to know why.

I was mysti-fucken'-fied.

"Because of you," she said. "I love George W. Bush because of you and people like you." Her eyes sparkled, she crossed her legs, and leaned in toward me, smiling, beautiful. "What did you know about my religion before Bush? What did you know of me and my people?"

This time she waited for me to say something, but again, she already knew the answer.

"I knew jackshit," I said.

"Jackshit means nothing, yes?"

"Yes."

"See? This is why I love the man. You Americans knew your jackshit about Muslims before Bush. This is why I love him." She laughed, satisfied and exuberant. She is 100 percent right. I knew very little of Islam or Muslims before Bush failed to recognize himself as satan in his fucked-up biblical prophecy.

And so, I have come to see more and more of the complexities of war.

In my daily life, I firmly believe that everything that happens serves a larger purpose. Often, I have no clue what this purpose might be, and I do not question it. If my neighbor's dog is barking incessantly, maybe I am being given a lesson in forbearance. Perhaps it is a lesson in getting involved with my neighbors and asking them if I can walk their dog in the afternoons when I am home. In the daily-life scheme of things, I really don't suffer much curiosity. I just listen to what the world might be saying and respond the best way I know how.

But for big things, like war, it is difficult to divine the lesson. The larger purpose in millions of people's lives being destroyed by violence eluded me. Until I started teaching refugees and became close with a family from Iraq.

Ali and Iman came to the US from Baghdad after their oldest son, Ammar, caught a stray bullet in his head. With their other three children—Zahara, Ghaith, and Anmar—in tow, they arrived in Seattle, Washington, in hopes of getting the bullet taken out of Ammar's head.

The organization I work for gave the family a home and hooked them up with English classes. The Jackass Organization that sponsored them was supposed to do everything else.

Well, they did jackshit. The JO seems to be one of many organizations that cashed in on Bush's faith-based initiative policies, for I understand that the JO got government funding for making it look like they were helping Iraqis, but no help was actually ever given. Later on, the JO reported Ali and Iman to a collection agency to recover the costs of the family's flight from Syria to Seattle.

In any case, my boss picked Ali and Iman up and brought them to class for two months, which is when I met them. After two months, though, we started getting a bunch of new refugees, and he could no longer taxi them to and from school. The public bus ride involved three transfers, and with two small children and a lack of understanding of the language and culture here, this was just not possible.

I called the JO a number of times on Ali and Iman's behalf. They needed a phone, they needed to get on welfare, they needed food stamps and towels and clothes for the kids.

The employees I spoke with were always doing their best, and it was obvious they were overworked and understaffed. One of the people trying to help the family ended up quitting in tears.

I could not bear the thought of this beautiful family being left to the wind and, in conjunction with my wife, Misty Tenderlove, took them to the welfare office and all the other places they needed to go. A friend of ours was deeply moved by their predicament and gave them lamps, rugs, boys clothes, and a two-hundred-dollar gift card. Another friend gave them top quality toys, girls clothes, and shoes.

I work at the refugee office during the day, so Misty Tenderlove took them to all of Ammar's medical appointments and eventually to the hospital for his surgery, which—along with all of their medical and subsistence costs—was covered by welfare.

The doctors said that the bullet in Ammar's head could not be removed. Brain tissue had grown around it and turned it into an oystery pearl. He would survive with the bullet intact, and to mess with it at this point would be dangerous.

This is where I started marveling at the endlessly complex scenarios that can and do unfold because of great violence. For, you see, in checking out the bullet, the doctors found a cyst in Ammar's head that would have killed him before he turned fifteen, giving the child less than six years to live.

They traveled thousands of miles, with four children and six suitcases representing the lives they had always known, and displaced themselves to the country that had destroyed their home to get a bullet taken out. But the bullet from this brutal occupation saved their child's life. Ali and Iman knew about the bump in his head. He had been born with it. They would have never sought out medical attention for the cyst.

The
bullet
saved
his
life.

Through translators, Misty Tenderlove convinced Ali and Iman that the bullet was not a problem, but that this heretofore unconsidered cyst would kill their beloved child. She took them to the hospital for the surgery. She prayed from the Koran with them while they waited. Iman trembled, staring, crying, chanting for hours. Ali held the Koran in his lap and prayed aloud. A soldier in uniform came into the waiting room and post-traumatic stress disorder kicked in in full force.

It was a hard day.

In the end, Ammar was okay.

He is alive because of this great violence.

Try and wrap your mind around that one because I have known for a few years now and my mind is still not fully wrapped.

After this, Iman and Zahara no longer wore their hijabs around us. We became family.

This great violence also introduced me to the Iraqi bread staple, khobz.

Pretty much the second they hit US soil, Iman was making khobz. She might be displaced, she might be scared, and she might be terrified about the welfare of her children and husband, but the most important thing in the whole wide world was making this wonderful bread.

I now believe that Ali would flounder if he did not have his khobz.

In class, she would feed her youngest children, Anmar and

Ghaith, with pieces of home-cooked chicken or cucumbers (or both) wrapped in torn pieces of this very interesting-looking bread.

I asked her about it, and she pulled out a gigantic piece of flatbread—huge and round, like a medium pizza. It was moist and delicious, bubbled thick in some places and crispy thin in others. Iman offered me a piece rolled around some cucumber, and I had never tasted such a wonderful single bread food in my life.

My first thought after that first amazing savory bite was, "How much has this bread cost?"

Gold-infused frozen hot chocolate with hidden diamond engagement rings cannot compare. I have tasted some of the dearest, most costly food in the world. Iman paid so very much to share this bread with me.

It cost her the destruction of her country, the loss of family members—some by death, some by unknown fate in Abu Ghraib prison. She was brutalized, she dodged bullets while pregnant, she watched her mosques desecrated and was helpless to do anything about any of it. Her son, shot in the head.

Very expensive bread.

Many foods we enjoy cost people dearly. Vietnamese, Korean, Jewish, Guatemalan, Nepalese, Tibetan, Persian, Ethiopian, and Japanese cuisines are all a part of the US eating experience. The people who brought it here did so at a great price. Great violence has made the US the best place on the planet to grab a bite to eat.

As much as violent histories make possible the destruction Iman has seen, they have also made possible these new understandings and relationships in our lives. It is painful to admit that my country's brutal occupation of Iraq led to one of the most beautiful relationships I have ever known. It is painful to know that this brutal occupation ultimately saved Ammar's life. But this, indeed, is the case. There are millions of beautiful hapa kids in the US, given life because of our choices in Vietnam, Japan, Hawaii, and Korea. War and brutal occupations bring many consequences, and not all of them are negative. It boggles my mind to recognize this, but it is true.

I might not be gracing the planet if it weren't for war. My mother's mother had an affair with an Irish soldier and got pregnant. If it weren't for Hitler's war, there would have been no need for soldiers in London, and so, no affair would have taken place. As much as great violence tears people apart, it also brings them together.

And I know there will come a time in the future when people in the US know the taste of khobz like we know the taste of Kim Chee and Phö.

War brings life and food. War brings post-traumatic stress disorder, rape, and flashbacks. War mixes up races and religions. War causes domestic violence. War is the single greatest intermingling force on the planet. Without wars, the world would be a lot more insular and ignorant.

Accepting this assists in an understanding of violence, great and small.

By examining the overall consequences of great violence, we can more clearly identify our individual and collective place in all of this. As it stands, our culture is arguably more accepting of the violence that comes with war and brutal occupations than it is of the delicious cuisines that they bring.

If one three hundredth of the present US population—that is, a million people—are allowing their young kids to play the video games *Vice* or *Grand Theft Auto*, where players get points for tearing through a cityscape stealing, raping women, and causing mayhem, that means that at a bare minimum one million kids are growing up learning that violence is rewarding.

Media producers love this argument: "It's not *our* fault kids love these games. It's not *our* fault there's a market for racist, violent movies and teevee shows. We're just filling a niche."

Well, that "niche" was created over many years of condoning violence and various crimes against humanity.

I recently received an e-mail from a young woman named Jacqueline Emathinger who is focusing on violent video games as a human rights issue. She told me about a Japanese game called *Rapelay*, which makes the rape scenes in *Grand Theft Auto* appear quaint.

The game (made by Illusion Soft, a company located in Yokohama) belongs to a genre called hentai, which roughly means "sexual perversion." These games regularly feature pornography and violent sex.

As you play, the story unfolds.

You are a young, wealthy man who was convicted of groping a young girl named Aoi on a train. Your parents bribed officials, and you got out of jail. You decide your best bet in life at this point is to hunt down Aoi, her younger sister (Manaka), and their mother (Yuuko). The object is to rape the women so many times that they become your sexual slaves. Keep in mind that the graphics in this game are pristine, and the rape looks quite real. As you rape each of the family members, their "arousal" level increases. They do not like being raped at first but eventually end up having orgasms. The manly folklore (manlore?) that women actually quite enjoy being raped is thus tidily served.

Manaka, by the way, is around eleven years old, so there's a pedophile edge there for anyone who enjoys that.

There are two "dangers" in the game. The first is if you rape Aoi in a certain sexual position before you have successfully broken her will, she will stab you to death. The second is if you get Aoi or Manaka pregnant without forcing them to have an abortion and either of them gives birth, they will push you in front of a train rather than have you be a part of their child's life. This is an easy pitfall to avoid, as you can plainly see their growing bellies as you rape them and have ample time to force an abortion.

These are the only "dangers" for you, the rapist. You never have to worry about the police or getting in trouble for doing something wrong, for evidently, you are not doing anything wrong. You are free to rape the women until the end of time. If you progress far enough in the game, you can invite other male characters to join you in various gang rape scenarios.

What

great

fun.

It takes a few minutes to download the uncensored English version of *Rapelay*, and here is how it is done:

Google "rapelay download."

Hit return.

Pick a link.

Hit the download button.

I've never stood by politicians who want to ban certain music or video games. If you want your kid to get a nasty burn, be sure to *ban* her from touching the cookies while they cool, you know what I'm saying? Banning makes something illicit. Illicit things have been popular with humanity since Eve ate a shiny red apple.

A great way to make something popular is to create a bunch of taboo around it.

Apples are the number one fruit in the US.

Instead, I am interested in the *thinking* behind media such as *Rapelay*. People sat in a room and discussed this video game at great,

great length. It was decided there was a big market for a graphic rape simulation game.

Who is this market?

Young boys and men.

Why would young boys and men enjoy raping women as a pastime? Because they feel powerless and impotent to change their reality! Wheee!

The money will roll right in.

I don't know if the people at Illusion Soft really spent a lot of time wondering what would *happen* to someone who virtually enacted rape repeatedly, hour after hour. There is no way to partake in and/or bear witness to dehumanization on this level without losing some of your own humanity.

Lose enough of your humanity and you are capable of committing or taking part in pretty much any atrocity.

The Mexican drug cartels know this trick.

Young men in Ciudad Juárez are forced to take part in the gang rape and murder of young women. Since the early 1990s, when NAFTA brought factories to this border town, thousands of women factory workers have disappeared. When a young man has taken part in and witnessed enough rape and murder, he is given the nipple of a dead girl. This he wears on a chain around his neck as an amulet to ward off powerlessness and impotence to change his reality.

He will follow any order at this point.

I know this because I had seen the strange shriveled meat-looking pendant in Juárez and wondered what the fuck it was. Then, auspiciously, the day after I got home from that trip, I went to a screening of a brilliant documentary by Lourdes Trujillo about the Juárez rapes and murders called *Señorita Extraviada*. The nipple pendant was discussed in the film, which you should be watching soon.

Militaries know this trick too.

Various rape tactics have also been used in Poland, France, Germany, Russia, Vietnam, Nicaragua, El Salvador, Colombia, Sudan, Rwanda, and Bosnia, thus robbing entire generations of young men of any sense of empathy.

Lose enough empathy and you become a bona fide sociopath, which is a great thing for a soldier. Sociopaths under command will undoubtedly follow orders. Trouble is, the young men, robbed of empathy, come home and raise the next generation.

Some of these men are our great-grandfathers, grandfathers, fathers, and brothers. One must wonder what kind of hell their children were raised in if their pop's empathy was destroyed. One doesn't need to wonder what kind of *cultural* hell is created by entire generations of men losing their empathy. It's on plain view every time we listen to the day's news.

The people who create video games for kids have normal human fears, dreams, insecurities, obsessions, resentments, and political views, all of which will undoubtedly be collectively reflected in the intimate world they create. You cannot create without contributing something of yourself—even if you are creating something with the marketing possibilities at the forefront of your consciousness.

Video games are worlds made by people.

People write the stories, create the characters, and foment seemingly endless scenarios. Individuals—a handful of individuals, really—create video games. They are often brilliant at what they do, and what they do is godlike.

Who else but god can create an alternate world in which your twelve-year-old can exist?

Not surprisingly, the US military uses video games to condition young people to kill. The military has opened up Army Experience Centers in malls throughout the nation because free high-end video arcades are much more effective at recruiting young people than traditional recruitment offices.

After Wikileaks posted a video of US soldiers shooting down innocent civilians in Iraq in 2010, many commentators noted how the soldiers sounded just like kids playing video games while they slaughtered children like Ammar and Zahara.

Because it is such a good medium for various simulations, pretty much forty-five seconds after the video game was invented, violence and rape were factored into this new technology. *Pong* was nonviolent, but from there on out, it was all about shooting down planets and eating dots and ghosts. One of the earliest pornographic games, *Custer's Revenge*, came out in 1982, a mere two years after *Pac-Man* made its debut. Here we have our intrepid player, as General George Custer, wearing a cavalry hat, a huge erection, and cowboy boots. Custer's objective (that is, revenge) is to rape an indian woman tied to a pole, while avoiding arrows and other pitfalls.

I read one review of *Rapelay* where the author, citing *Custer's Revenge*, reminisced about the simpler times of video games.

Harkening back to the simplicity of the past is an ongoing theme of humanity's, while we obsess over progress and the constant sensation of "moving forward."

Progress compared to what?

Moving forward to where?

Ventures that pull us further away from our humanity and from nature are regularly defended as "advancements." Take, for example, iPhones, deep-water drilling, mountaintop removal, nuclear physics, and electronic cat-shit boxes that utilize motion-censored sweepers to keep our hands from ever coming into contact with the nastiness from our pets' asses.

Wars are seen as advanced too, and the more removed a person is from the actual death of another human being or ecosystem, the more technologically advanced their military is perceived to be. Our constant "advancements" are moving us further and further away from our own humanity, making it easier and easier for us all to participate in some very serious atrocities.

In olden times, like today, war was a business. It wasn't as streamlined as it is now, but it was almost always about someone wanting to take something from somebody else to get money, power, resources, land, or all of the above.

Twenty-five hundred years ago a military strategist named Sun Tzu wrote *The Art of War*. It has been published the world over pretty much ever since it was written. There are many editions of this text, and a lot of them are geared toward corporate folk. Though these editions definitely serve a purpose—anyone wishing to get a firmer hold on their understanding of the global corporatocracy should have one—I like the hippee Shambhala version best.

Here is how the jacket of that edition sums up *The Art of War*.

> Conflict is an inevitable part of life, according to this ancient Chinese classic of strategy, but everything necessary to deal with conflict wisely, honorably, victoriously, is right before us at all times. The key to skillful action in any situation is in knowing those things that make up the environment and then arranging them so that their power becomes available to us. It is not necessary to change the nature of things to come to victory. Crucial to Sun Tzu's vision is knowledge—especially self-knowledge—and a view

of the whole that seeks to bring the conflicting views around to a vision of the larger perspective.

I mean, people get pissed off all the time. You gotta figure it's part of human nature or, actually, the natural order, since animals get pissed off too. But when you grow up in a society where it's normal to pretend bad things don't happen and where it's a sign of weakness to show emotion, it's up to you to teach yourself how to handle conflict. That's where *The Art of War* comes in. Even if you don't understand it, still, keep reading it. I don't understand a quarter of it, but the spirit of the book seeps into my understanding and helps me to deal, osmosis-style.

The Art of War describes rules of engagement and strategies for overcoming various adversaries. Because most societies are modeled upon the premise of (and often a natural proclivity toward) war, this book reflects power, economy, and cultural structures found the world over. These are largely organized around hierarchies and rectangles.

More on hierarchies and rectangles later.

The Art of War has a lot to offer those who seek to understand how to live and love in this violent time.

There are a lot of theories about why people wage war. Some believe that mentally unstable leaders compel their citizens to corroborate or validate their insanity by killing/being killed at said leader's behest:

If war is innate to human nature, as is presupposed and predetermined (according to determinism philosophy) by many psychological theories, then there is little hope of ever escaping it. Psychologists have argued that while human temperament allows wars to occur, this only happens when mentally unbalanced people are in control of a nation. This school of thought argues leaders that seek war such as Napoleon, Hitler, Osama bin Laden, Saddam Hussein, and Stalin [Why is George W. Bush not on this list and why do wikipedians erase his name whenever I add it?] were mentally abnormal, but fails to explain the thousands of free and presumably sane people who wage wars at their behest. Some psychologists argue that such leaders are a manifestation of the build up of anger and madness repressed in modern societies and it is only they that are allowed to show various mental anomalies. Because people elect and support such leaders suggestions have been made that very few people are in fact sane and that modern society is an unhealthy one. Scientists such as Desmond Morris have argued that stress is the major cause of death in people of today. Heart failure, obesity, mental disorders and long lists of diseases are proven to be related to stress. Therefore showing that the rise of insane leaders is due to a very toxic environment in which presumably healthy individuals exist and that social pressure forces mentally healthy people to participate in conflicts. (http:/psychology.wikia.com/wiki/war)

In this way of thinking, we're all crazy due to stress. I'd qualify this. Most of us living under the high-tech stress of modern civilization are detached from the earth, our selves, one another, and humanity in general and are therefore emotionally immature. We are desensitized to destruction and violence, so we can hardly witness its significance. We forget what is valuable. We disrespect ourselves and others. Moreover, we haven't had four generations of peace to get ourselves straight in the head or the heart.

The two worst things I ever did to other people were because of low self-esteem—because I didn't know where I belonged in the world or why my life was valuable.

The first was when I was a freshman in high school. In junior high, my place was secure, but when I entered high school, I didn't know where I belonged. Some of my friends from junior high became street rats—the kids who hung out in the school parking lot—and some became popular girls. I didn't want to be a street rat, so I hung out with the popular girls. Until one day, when my friends and I found out that an older popular girl had made out with Christy Todd's boyfriend at a party. We vandalized the entire school with insults directed at the older popular girl. We didn't realize how seriously epic our actions were until we'd covered the entire campus with horrible things. When we got in trouble for it, my popular friends decided their best recourse for surviving the next few years of high school was to kiss the asses of *all* the older popular girl's friends. I wasn't up for that, so I was pretty much on my own until I met the punk rockers. This vandalism really ruined that older popular girl's life for a while. I would have apologized to her at the time if it didn't mean kissing the asses of an entire group of people until they graduated. But it was a very shitty thing to do, and I probably wouldn't have done it if I had felt that there was a place in the world for me.

The other thing I did was when I was older, after my first book, *Cunt*, came out. I'd spent four years working on it, holding down various jobs, and I had no other life. When *Cunt* was finished, I was at a loss about what to do and again felt there was no place for me in the world. Around this time, I met up with an old friend who was in a relationship. We became lovers, and it broke up the relationship. I totally disrespected someone's relationship because I felt lowly about myself.

What a shitty thing to do.

This is why self-esteem is so important. We tend to lack empathy and caring for others when we have none for ourselves.

My Uncle Bruce used to raise fighting cocks. He refers to this period of his life as "the wealthiest I ever was."

In one of my father's many questionable parenting calls, he took me to the cockfights when I was four or five. I do not have a clear memory of this time, and I was too small to see past the crush of humanity crowded around the walls enclosing the fight ring. I do, however, remember the smell of blood. And I remember the excitement. And I can still taste the terror in my mouth. Whether it was my terror or the cock's terror, I don't know. My father realized his huge mistake, not necessarily of having exposed a small child to a down and dirty cockfight, but for bringing on the fall-out: an endless onslaught of questions persisting for many years. Why do people pay money to see chickens die violent deaths? Why do the roosters fight? Who thought of this? Why is it so popular? Why did you tell me not to tell Mom you took me there?

I don't remember his answers to any of these questions, but I never forgot that violence and, worse, how everyone around me embraced it with high-stakes gusto. It is a metaphor that has been endlessly replicated throughout my life.

One of our jobs as human beings is to learn to condone and accept violence as inevitable. Sometimes we condone it in our homes and sometimes we accept it in the world, but by the time we get to be fifteen years old, violence, of almost any kind, is "just the way things are."

It is *naïve* to question violence.

History *is* history because it involves various acts of violence—or the signing of decrees, which were brought about through violence. Almost any historic event can be traced to violence. Betsy Ross sitting on the porch, sipping iced tea, and sewing the flag? Each star and stripe represented land and culture stolen from murdered, sickened, and raped indians. Also, thousands of patriots and British soldiers died so that Betsy could sew her flag. Whether or not this Betsy and the flag business ever happened is questionable, but the story has taken on a life of its own, and like many historical happenings, it doesn't matter whether Betsy actually sewed the flag or not. Kids are taught the Betsy story in schools, and for various reasons it serves the victors of history's present telling, so there you have it.

Most things that allegedly happened—from the creation of the universe according to white men with big telescopes, to stolen, fraudulent elections—came about because of violence in one form or another.

We recognize certain acts as violence. Others, we don't even notice. Then there are the acts of passive violence that occur, and we call them many, many other things, like hanging chads, supply and demand, Proposition 8, office-place gossip, or just the way the cookie crumbles.

This is what interests me greatly: the sheer *volume* of violence that—because of mainstream designations and other value judgments—is not acknowledged as violence at all.

I think if we took a look at all the types of violence we don't really recognize, we would learn a lot about ourselves and the culture surrounding us.

Violence of any kind—passive or physical—requires a predator and prey. Think of all the contexts in which a predator and prey occur: Type A shoppers, ramming their cart down the aisle, barely missing your kindergartener. Speeding drivers endangering the lives of bicyclists with every reckless turn. Developers, studying blueprints of your neighborhood, coercing old folks to sell their beloved homes to make room for beige condos with hunter green trim. Churches that shake people down for money in the name of salvation. (Does it truly require three mansions and a full-time staff to serve the lord?) Predatory lending rates require prey. The weight loss, entertainment, and fashion industries prey on the insecurities indoctrinated around femininity. The sports industry, industrial-military, and industrial-prison complexes prey on the insecurities indoctrinated around masculinity. And we can't forget the police who sit on my block, waiting for one of the underage black kids in the park to light up a cigarette or do anything that can be construed as illegal. Even though they spend far more time scoping out the park than I do, they can't seem to tell which kids are corner drug clerks and which ones just got out of school and are hanging out with their friends. They're all black, they're all young, and they're all in the park. Therefore they're all going to be arrested if they make one misstep.

These forms of violence, even if acknowledged, are considered relatively unremarkable.

Even murder is not uniformly considered remarkable violence. The murder of anything other than human beings is unremarkable. For instance, old-growth forests, all life in the Gulf of Mexico, and the migratory Magnolia Warbler don't matter. Mass murder of humans is *generally* not acceptable, especially if it takes place in a wealthy and/or frontier nation. But people get slaughtered in Africa all the time, and it barely musters an e-mail petition. Mass murder is mostly okey-dokey if it's called "war" or if it's poor people and/or people of color who are doing the dying.

It largely depends on who is killed and who does the killing.

People who happen to live in the right location and who have the right identity and finances get away with murder all the time. If you are a member of the Israeli armed forces, you can murder Palestinian people with impunity. However, if you are Palestinian and you murder an Israeli, you're a terrorist. Wealthy white folks in the United States have been getting away with murder for five hundred years, so when a wealthy black man got acquitted for killing his ex-wife and her alleged romantic interest, it seemed like something of a triumph to many of the folks who have been getting murdered by white men for centuries—even those who were morally repelled by this crime.

Oprah is one of a few powerful individuals who affect US culture by proactively fighting to remove our blinders when it comes to violence in America.

She did a show once on a child-porn sting where police ended up busting an eighteen-year-old boy. At first they thought it was his father they were after because people—even jaded police officers—still have a hard time wrapping their minds around the utter pandemic of sexual terrorism in our environment/culture. They had seized the kid's child-porn collection, and when the arresting officers came on the program, Oprah wanted to show some excerpts for the exact same reason she insisted that New Orleans officials allow her and her cameras into the Superdome after Hurricane Katrina. "People *lived* this shit," Oprah said (I paraphrase). "Why the hell shouldn't I and others, at the very least, bear witness to their trauma?"

She was informed that it was illegal to show footage of the child porn, so she settled for graphic descriptions from the police.

In one video, a little girl is forced to give a dog a blow job while two other children watch.

In another, a man rapes a little child on a dirty bed.

The police officer—the one in charge of the sting—never referred to these incidents as "molestation," "incest," "oral sex," or "sexual engagement." She called them what they are: rape.

Repeatedly and definitively.

I loved her for that.

Oprah was all, "You know, maybe this is deeply unpleasant for you to hear about, much less see, *but how do you think that child feels?*"

How can anyone *allow* a child to have such a horrible experience completely alone in the world?

If the environment/culture maintains its ignorance about this horror show, then our children are, by and large, experiencing rape alone.

Why would *anyone* choose to luxuriate in ignorance while children are being treated this way throughout the world and in our own neighborhood or family?

This is, after all, our world. We all live in it together. It is a reflection of our most intimate selves. I may be getting all anthropological n' shit, but it does not reflect well on *anyone* who lives in a culture when kids get raped.

Our culture *produces* domestic violence, psychopathic murderers, child rapists, recess bullies, and freeway sociopaths. These kinds of predators organically result from many factors that describe our culture: self-absorption, unwillingness to deal with abuse, lack of resources to help people with their problems, lack of empathy, bloated senses of entitlement, survival of the fittest, lying, cheating, and stealing. These are just a few of many mundane realities found in our frontier culture/environment.

Of course we produce serial killers and child rapists.

Examining our culture/environment and understanding how and why we produce such individuals is therefore key. Holding ourselves accountable for the violence we perpetuate goes hand in hand with this examination. Ultimately, a restructuring of our frontier-minded culture and cultural identity is in order.

Chapter 2: **The Violence of Entitlement**

In olden times, empires rose and fell. Like one big, long-assed breath, with a lot of dead bodies and fancy dress balls in between.

They were run by one ruling fella—yer Julius Caesar, Constantine type. Empire building was a violent business, I think we can all agree on that. When yer Constantine decided to bring civilization and conquering to your land, that meant soldiers, rape, murder. It's impossible to impose alien renditions of god, economics, culture, and political infrastructure without a tsunami of bloodshed.

And don't forget about the looting n' pillaging.

Empire building inspired an awful lot of violence.

In empire times, one ruling man forcefully thrust his specific vision about everything, from city planning (where the native folks who survived lived in slums designed by architects of the new empire) to new job descriptions (where everyone who looked like the civilization-bringer was the boss over everyone who didn't). The Constantines had certain ideas about how life should be lived, and they made sure everyone in their self-projected path had a fabulously vivid understanding of those ideas.

Today, Bill Gates does not ride into battle against tattooed blue men. Howard Schultz does not rape the daughters of kings. The Walton family does not burn towns to the ground.

We live in kinder, gentler times.

Past civilizations were honest about what they were up to. "We're the fucken' Spaniards, man, and we're gonna control all the trade routes and gold supplies on the planet, and you can kiss our randy indian-raping asses if you think otherwise."

Now, it's more like, "Oh, hi! We're the Walton family! We're here to offer jobs to your community! We're here to make yer little world a better place! Oh, what's that you say? Your grandfather committed suicide because we rendered his tire store obsolete? Well, obviously he wasn't as committed to serving the community as we are. What's that you say? We don't offer health insurance? Well, go on down to the welfare office and get some medical coupons. The state government is as committed to us serving your community as we are! It's all good, toots!"

Or, "Hi! We want to bring jobs and industry to your poor nation! We really love your country, and if you'll just remove those pesky child labor laws and let us own your water supply, we think you will look pretty appetizing to our shareholders. What's good for business is good for everyone in the world! Yippee!"

The idea is the same now as it was in olden times: nothing has value unless it benefits the men who rule. The earth, animals, people of color, and white women are still resources within the business venture. It has always been this way with this man. He always has to one-up his daddy. I do not know why this is so important to him.

In the twenty-first century, after lots of "advancements," he controls the world from his corner window office and is home in time for dinner.

Here are some examples of economic entitlement violence at work:

Need coal?

Blow the muthafucken' tops of the mountains off!

Need water?

Brand it, take control of a region's water supply, and have a very Nestlé day!

Need oil?

Vampiristically suck the earth's blood out! Who *cares* if the oil is what keeps the earth's plates from rubbing together and causing catastrophic earthquakes! Who *cares* if it destroys the land and life in Nigeria and the Gulf Coast region?

Need tomatoes?

Enslave undocumented workers, bioengineer the bitches, and celebrate when the US judicial system says you have a right to patent seeds! Be sure to strong-arm any small-time farmer who has land you want!

Need milk?

Impregnate them heifers and keep 'em in a constant hormonal nightmare for their entire lives! Take their babies and put them in miniscule cages from birth to death! Their meat is called veal, and folks just love it!

According to Bill Gates's *Encarta World English Dictionary*, "entitle" means to "grant somebody right," "give title to something," and my favorite, to "award somebody honor." All of these definitions, you might note, involve someone *bequeathing* entitlement to someone or something else.

In live action, entitlement involves someone taking what they believe to be theirs. It's difficult to conceptualize the "honor" folks may have for white men who show up with guns and deeds and proclamations about how life is gonna be until they take everything they want and decide it's time to leave.

This sense of colonial-based entitlement is modeled in countless ways throughout daily life: loud cell phone conversations in public places, corporate takeovers, rampage killings, not stopping for pedestrians, shoving, stampeding, even trampling people to death in stores, bullying (including the ever winsome cyber bullying, which has inspired children to commit suicide), and countless microwars of many kinds.

Here is an example of how entitlement plays out in the US.

Bristow, Oklahoma, is a small town like many towns.

My cousin grew up there, after a six-year stint in Santa Maria. She liked Bristow well enough, with its jewelry store, clothing shops, cafés, a hardware store, drugstore, and all the other little local businesses that make a small town a self-sustaining economic ecosystem.

And then Wal-Mart invaded and colonized and homogenized the little town of Bristow. The government and Wal-Mart are great friends. Numerous federal laws, loopholes, and corrupt kickbacks pad Wal-Mart's coffers, as they set about destroying pristine little local communities such as Bristow.

As the businesses closed, a ghost town took its place: shuttered windows, plywood storefronts. Everyone was forced to shop at Wal-Mart, where every product is made in China. *All money flows out of the local community and out of the country.* Every product is identical in every Wal-Mart in every town across the nation.

Then Super Wal-Mart dropped a bomb on little Bristow. The

regular Wal-Mart would be closing, leaving a corrugated steel carcass and acres of drought-causing pavement behind. When the US dropped atomic bombs on Japan, "Little Boy" stripped Hiroshima, and three days later, "Fat Man" obliterated Nagasaki.

This is kinda like that.

Super Wal-Mart offers bioengineered Monsanto-sourced robo-food, evil-pharmaceutical corporation drugs, and cut-rate medical care via Wal-Mart doctors.

The only jobs available are through Wal-Mart, which has an agreement with the government about health care. Wal-Mart agrees to pay their employees little enough so that they are eligible for medical coupons. The US government and taxpayers, then, pay for Wal-Mart's employee health program.

You know that stereotype of the welfare mother? She's usually black, lazy, and entirely unambitious. Well, this little lady would be hard pressed to compete with Wal-Mart.

This doesn't look like a brutal occupation, given the slow death of broken spirits, and it doesn't smell like an occupation, so long as you avoid wandering around what used to be your town, and it doesn't sound like an occupation, unless someone documented each scene in each family's home when they realized Wal-Mart had destroyed their livelihood and edited it all into a time-lapse documentary.

Nonetheless, it is a brutal occupation.

The result is a conquered land and a colonized and—what is most damaging—deeply assimilated population. Many folks do, after all, *love* Wal-Mart and would defend the very thing that destroyed their community with their last dying breath.

This is presently one of the hallmarks of people in the US: we demand politicians who are going to fuck us over, and we fight for the right to be shafted by corporations.

We actively partake in our own abuse and demise as a civilization.

We think of this as "moving forward."

It's not exactly fun to think about all of these occupations based on entitlement, but it is quite nice to recognize it for what it is and then figure out one's next move from there à la *Art of War*. I don't shop at Wal-Mart, but that is because I have the luxury of living in a place where there are plenty of other options. If I had no recourse, I would probably fight to get Wal-Mart out of my community, as many, many people have throughout the years. People such as Al Norman of Sprawl-Busters, Charles Smith of Wal-Ocaust and Wal-Qaeda T-shirt fame, the glorious souls at WalMartWatch.com, and Teamsters and Raging Grannies pretty much everywhere.

People in Mexico, Canada, and the UK are none too pleased with Wal-Mart, either.

There's no Constantine here. The US is, instead, an intricate series of microempires, and the visions we forcefully thrust on others are generally considered to be nonviolent, friendly sounding things like "free markets" and "globalization."

All the same, we have a genetic past that we can't (or don't want to) shake, which promotes new and improved forms of invading and colonizing.

Here in the US we rose magnificently and are presently falling in the manner of olden-time empires.

Five hundred years ago, up until the last half century or so, god hated black people and indians in the US of A.

Now he hates fags.

Depending on who you talk to, god also hates feminists and a vast, infinitely complex population of people known as "Middle Easterners." Israelis are, by way of geographic reality, Middle Easterners, but they are not *called* Middle Easterners, so god doesn't include them.

In the US, god's hatred is closely linked with the imagination and collective consciousness of white Christians.

His hatred works in mysterious ways.

In many countries, including my own, god's hatred settles on women—those who do not cloak themselves according to his will, those who are raped, those who have no husband. God has been known to hate children born into devastating poverty, whoever happens to be indigenous, and those caught in the middle of a war.

Again, depending on whom you talk to, god hates Tibetans, Americans, Haitians, and Palestinians. Hindus, Muslims, Christians, 'n' Jews.

But almost everyone everywhere can agree on one thing: god hates fags.

Originally, the US empire started with religion. Today, various forms of Christianity still dominate the collective consciousness and defend these ventures.

This is because the folks who "founded" the country were Christian, and the god-who-hates-fags often speaks to them. The Bible informs most Christians, and the Bible (Genesis 1:26, to be exact) says it's okey-dokey to commit untold atrocities against indians and black people:

> And God said, Let us make man in our image, after our likeness: and let them have dominion over the fish of the sea, and over the fowl of the air, and over the cattle, and over all the earth, and over every creeping thing that creepeth upon the earth.

If you have a hard time seeing the part about god sanctioning a centuries-long indian holocaust and five hundred years of slavery, well, our forebears didn't. Only white Christians were considered to be "man in our image."

Indians, Africans, noncompliant whites, and eventually, African-

Americans were lumped in with "every creeping thing that creepeth upon the earth." I deduce this based on three factors: indians, slaves, and noncompliant whites and black folks weren't fish, and they did not fly or moo.

Hence, the ease of mind in writing important sentences that say stuff like, "All men are created equal."

The idea people were getting from this Bible god was that they should claim dominion over everything that moved. This idea chaperoned the indian holocaust, slavery, and pretty much every atrocity since, right up to droning Afghan people to death.

Without god's hatred to back folks up, whites would have been like, "Whoa, we're killin' an awful lot of people and buffalo here, don't cha think?" But since Manifest Destiny was *ordained* by god, well dang, white folks simply had *no say* in the matter. "Our hands are tied! It's not our fault god loves us best."

A lot more people would have said, "I dunno, Dad, maybe it's kinda wrong for us to be raping these women every night and selling their children and humiliating their men in every conceivable manner." But god said they weren't *really* women, children, and men so committing atrocities against them was actually *part* of getting through the pearly gates.

You don't wanna be tinkerin' with the will-o-god.

And so, too, organized religion escorted these crimes against humanity to the cotillion of US history.

Without denial of the indian holocaust and slavery, the violence that presently exists in the Americas could not sustain itself.

And the history of violence rages on.

We also learn special animosities from our families and lug them around our hearts. My mother comes from Irish Republican Army people. The ones who aren't very pleased with the British or the Northern Irish who were exiled into Ireland from Scotland over five hundred years ago.

This forced exile, called the Ulster Plantation, happened in the early part of the 17th century, when the king of Scotland—wanting to make nice with Britain—uprooted a population of rabble-rousing marauders on the border the two countries shared, and thousands of people were shipped off to Northern Ireland. This, by the way, is where the word *plantation* comes from and also a wonderful example of how acts of great violence live on to procreate other acts of great violence. Hundreds of years later, many descendents from this replanted population, known as the Scots-Irish, relocated to the American colonies and created plantations in the South for slaves to labor on. So hundreds of years after suffering under the subjugation of an enforced plantation, Scots-Irish people themselves founded plantations and subjugated others. To this day, most Scots-Irish people in the South are from slave-owning families.

Whee!

No force on earth will ever truly convince me that Northern (Scots) Irish people belong in Ireland. Where, exactly, should the Northern Irish *go* after living in Ireland for hundreds of years?

Damned if I know.

I'm certainly parroting an idea that my mother taught me to believe when I was a kid, and no matter how many ways I look at the situation as an adult, I can't see a place for the Northern Irish people in Ireland. They cause nothing but problems with their Protestant elitism. Value judgments abound in my thinking here, and I make no apologies for them. I feel the exact same way about Israel in Palestine and white folks in the US. It's just not cool for people to show up on other people's land and start bossing everyone around.

Ye olde animosities are hardly ever rational, just, or even plausible. It is, though, an exceedingly good idea to make note of their existence and the special power they hold in our hearts.

Northern Irish and Israeli kids are raised hearing their parents say things that keep the animosities alive no less than Irish and Palestinian kids. When problems go back hundreds—sometimes thousands—of years, there is no middle ground, no diplomatic solution.

Nonetheless, it's imperative to look at old animosities for what they are and try to understand the other side's perspective. The Northern Irish were forced to move to Ireland against their will in the early 1600s. At some point, the people of Ireland have got to accept this reality. The Israelis were devastated after World War II. They needed a safe place, and the US and Britain didn't want them in their countries, so everyone suddenly remembered where the Israelis were during biblical times. It's deeply unfortunate that the Northern Irish and the Israelis don't seem to have the graciousness to live in peace with the people who were there before them, and it is deeply unfortunate that the Irish and Palestinians have resorted to violence, which hardly inspires ungracious people to act graciously, but fuck, man, it gets tiresome when someone has their boot in your face while setting fire to your five-hundred-year-old olive groves.

Tibet, China, India, Pakistan, Kashmir, Iraq, Iran, Russia, Chechnya, Georgia, Somalia, Ethiopia, Rwanda, Sudan, Bosnia, and Serbia all have histories rife with ancient animosities.

Think of all the children listening to their parents, absorbing one story into their hearts.

People were murdered, raped, enslaved, and beaten to create most nations, and this is especially true in the United States of America.

Those are our roots no less than the Declaration of Independence.

Present-day people in the US descend from this, but we are in no way equipped to deal with it because our violent history is manipulated and glossed over throughout our education. In an end-less cycle of indoctrination, we have normalized things that are pathologically abnormal. We are schooled to understand the indians were "removed" from their lands and that slavery was a few bad apples in Ye Olde South. *Unfortunate* things may have occurred on the journey of self-determination against the British throne, but the blood and sorrow of anyone who disagreed with the way things were going down is hardly worth consideration.

These lies we are told as children don't really serve us when we take a gander at our various places in the world. This denial we learn to lug around in our hearts debilitates us and prevents us from shifting the present power dynamic. It is costly and retards our growth as human beings.

I don't know why we hang onto it.

Today, it is difficult to get vast populations mobilized around the fate of the Brown Pelican, the coastal Redwood, or all life in the Gulf of Mexico because things of the earth are considered beneath us—part of a wilderness that god *explicitly directed us to tame and dominate.* Their destruction is sanctioned violence under a deluded mindset.

If you own the land, you own the people who labor on it. You own the birds that fly in your airspace and the fish that swim in your rivers. You are not a mere aspect of the world, oh no. Rather, you straddle it like it's your grumpy old nag, and you kick it in the stomach when it's not doing what you want.

Transocean is the shady US-based company that owns the Deepwater Horizon oil rig, which, at the time of this writing, is pumping about 210,000 gallons of oil into the gulf every day with no end in sight. The company was located in the *rigorously* regulated Cayman Islands before it took tax shelter in Switzerland. Newspapers love to call Transocean a Swiss company, but it's a US -based company and the local Swiss hate their guts.

How will Transocean and British Polluters even begin to compensate for this holocaust? They're much more concerned about the profits lost from the oil pouring into the ocean than anything else. I hope the people in the US, Mexico, and Cuba rise up against these shitstains together. But here, we're so conditioned to the idiocy of corporatocracy, we'll probably rest well with the appointment of a White House commission packed with oil industry lobbyists to investigate.

Mexico and Cuba might start some shit, but we here in the US probably won't have their backs.

We will go along with it 'cause, within the bounds of our indoctrination, it seems useless to worry about one little accident, and furthermore, we don't know how to do what Gandhi said and simply take to the streets.

And so, we, the people, seem to be accepting yet another atrocity.

This entitled mentality doesn't exist only in Fortune 500 tycoons. The really fascinating part of it all is that—to vastly varying degrees—entitlement lies in the hearts and souls of most everyone reared in a frontier nation. I hang out with refugees who do not have this sense of entitlement, and I must say, it is so nice to spend time away from it.

Our unchecked indoctrinated entitlement is very concerning.

I had a very intense experience with the peace movement that helped me to understand how the passive violence of entitlement deeply undermines our best intentions.

Not long after it became clear that our tax dollars for schools, education, welfare, libraries, transportation, and health care were to be squandered on military bombs, shyster contractors, and operations against the people of Afghanistan and Iraq, a woman named Parisha invited me to speak at a big march against the "war" in Washington, DC.

I wanted to do it, but it was hard to get excited. If we oppose these brutal occupations, let's oppose them for what they are, rather than what reptilian spin-lizards decided to call them.

Despite these lexical misgivings, I was of course honored to be invited to Washington DC, and I said yes. So Parisha signed me on and sent me an e-mail saying I would be staying at the Sheraton or Hilton or some other huge, global economy vampire that sucks revenue out of communities worldwide.

I was stunned that an antiwar organization would opt to funnel resources to multinational corporations over locally owned small businesses.

I was all, "Parisha, what's up with this? Are you all really opposing the bombing of Iraq while giving your money to a huge corporation over a small locally owned business?"

This is when Parisha came out as a bit of a maverick within the antiwar organization machine. She told me that she was the one who had really pushed to bring me there and that no one else really knew about my work or why she was so insistent on bringing me to the march.

So Parisha did some research. She found me a really cool, locally owned inn to stay at and channeled some Marriot- or Hilton-intended funds.

I got to the very cool little inn and was met by Shawna, the mistress of all trades on duty. She showed me to my room and directed me to a street where I'd find a buncha restaurants, and I had a nice evening stroll. I ended up at an Ethiopian restaurant and had a good dinner. On my way back, I passed a dark basement bar with a red light shining on a pool table. The place was named something sinister sounding, like the Dragon's Crypt or Beelzebub's Lair. Something like that. I was hesitant to go in because it's never seemed a good idea to go alone into an unknown bar in an unknown city. I had never, up to that point in my life, done such a thing.

But the way that red light was shining on that pool table, filling the window and spilling out onto the sidewalk compelled me. It beckoned like a candy store, a happy hooker, a swimming hole on a hot summer day.

Also, it felt auspicious and somehow right.

Despite my heretofore nonnegotiable self-defense tenets, I went into the Cryptic Lair, got a beer, and put my name on the chalkboard. There were eight or ten men, of various races and ages, crowded around the table. Not one other woman anywhere near the pool table.

Again, another no-no.

And again, I was surprised that my body was very relaxed, even though my mind was racing. I sensed that I was safe, though it was incredibly difficult to rationalize.

The men seemed to more or less know each other, and it was a friendly scene. I stood awkwardly off to the side for a few moments, until one of the men said, "Hey, I'm up next, you can have my seat."

I felt acknowledged and welcomed by this simple action.

I relaxed a bit more in my new seat with a great view of the table.

When it was my turn to play, I trounced my opponent. I beat three in a row before losing. The men started introducing themselves to me, and soon enough we got into a lively conversation. They were dockworkers, steel fabricators, mail deliverers, taxi drivers. They were very interested in *Cunt*, and we talked about the upcoming brutal occupation of Iraq, to which they were all opposed.

I spent a relaxing and thoroughly enjoyable three hours playing pool and totally hanging out with a group of men in a city I did not know.

When I wanted to go back to the inn, they said I shouldn't walk alone and elected someone to walk me back. Again, every rational self-defense fiber of my being bristled, but in my heart, I knew they were sincere and simply wished me to come to no harm late at night.

So one of them walked me to my inn and said good night and went back to the Cryptic Lair.

I woke up early the next day and made my way to Malcolm X Park, where the rally before the march was going to be held. I got there early because I wanted to see the park go from an empty space to a full space. I sat on a bench and watched people arrive; flowing scarves and banners as well as tents started to appear before my eyes. Huge contingents of people from all over the nation pulled up in their chartered buses. A stage went up, a PA. I watched the whole thing. It was really kinda beautiful. As the morning went on, I meandered to the area behind the stage and introduced myself to officials until I found Parisha. She told me I'd be going on just before the last speaker, which was perfect. My plan was to get everyone to scream, all at once, really loud, before marching off to the White House. I figured people would be filled up with words by all the speakers, and so instead of offering more words, I'd offer a chance to let off some of that accumulated energy. So I was pretty happy to learn I'd be going up close to the end.

There were a lot of important people arriving, and I wandered off into the crowd again. There was a "backstage" energy developing, and I was beginning to feel uncomfortable. In my experience, people start acting badly when there is a distinction made between those who are important and those who are the masses. World history is rife with examples of this reality, but moreover, I have been in the presence of important people enough to have noticed. When a hierarchy is in place, those who are designated important become impervious to the reality of others, and meanwhile, everyone else develops a yearning to be important too. This is why celebrities have stalkers and why there exists a perfectly legal industry where photographers stalk celebrities. People spend money, time, and energy engrossed in the lives of important people rather than being present in their own lives.

At the rally, entourages and stuff like that started to appear. The air tensed with the presence of celebrity, which somehow offers meaning and depth to everyone else's self-perceived meaningless and shallow existence.

It is so bizarre how people change when celebrity shows up.

And there was a lot of celebrity here.

I circled the whole rally again and returned to what was, officially, a backstage area. The antiwar officials looked at the pass Parisha had given me and told me not to leave the backstage area again. If I did, they wouldn't let me through. I was stunned. I'd been walking around the whole park for hours. It was how I was dealing with my nervousness about being on a stage in front of thousands of people. I needed to see the whole thing evolve in order to cope with the reality of standing in front of all those folks and really give them something from my heart. I was all, "Are you serious? I can't leave this area for the rest of the rally?" They said they were doing crowd control, and it was so difficult to keep people out of the backstage area where all the important people and their entourages were that they decided to just stop letting anyone through at all.

Too many people. Security reasons, sorry.

I figured, whatever.

I'd brought a few signed copies of *Cunt* that I wanted to give to three of the women who were speaking who had impacted my life and inspired me. Since I was now sequestered with the important people, it seemed a good opportunity to keep my eye out for the three women.

I located two of them easily enough. I told them they'd changed my life, said thanks, and gave them *Cunts*. They were both really nice, and it was good to meet them.

The third woman was a famous writer who had been a part of

my reading for over two decades. I loved her and was very excited to give her a copy of my book. Her writing had deeply inspired me throughout my life.

She was nowhere to be seen.

I stood by a wall, overlooking a large sunken garden. Soon enough, a cop walked up and stood next to me. We had said our hellos earlier in the morning and now struck up a conversation. We talked about the upcoming "war." We were not in agreement, but we respected each other's viewpoints. He and his wife were taking care of their three grandchildren while his son and daughter-in-law served in the military. His pain and worry were evident, and I suspected his support of the illegal occupation said more about his concern for his family than his opinion of the US government's ridiculous shenanigans. He thought the "war on terror" was highly problematic, and so his stance, like so many things, was complex.

He also talked a lot about the park. About its history. It had been his beat for over twenty-five years. Malcolm X Park was his park. The neighborhood, he told me, was in the process of being colonized by a wealthier, whiter class who wanted to change the park's name.

He was pretty outraged about that.

He got a call on his radio, and so we said our good-byes.

As he walked away, the strangest thing happened.

Three of those huge papier-mâché puppets that always appear at protests walked toward me from right, left, and center. They all just seemed to appear out of nowhere, right as the cop walked away. I was standing with my back to the wall still, facing the back of the stage and the huge crowd beyond, and these puppets are all walking toward me.

Then, the famous writer materialized.

She walked straight toward me and stopped four feet in front of me, right smack dab in the middle of all of the puppets. She turned to each one and bowed. The puppets all bowed to her. Then she walked to the wall and stood next to me.

It was like some dream or something. I could never in a million years anticipate a scene like that unfolding in front of me.

I turned to her and kinda nervously said, "Hello, famous writer. You have inspired me all of my life, and I brought a copy of my book for you."

I pulled it out of my bag and offered it to her.

She looked down at it like it was a piece of rotting, maggot-infused pork and she was a Muslim and said, "What am I supposed to do with that?"

I spluttered, "Uhm, I just wanted to give you a copy of my book."

"I don't have anywhere to put it," she spat at me, glaring. "Where do you expect me to put it?"

"I dunno," I said. "Uhm, sorry. Uh."

I put it back in my bag and walked away.

My heart was beating in my chest, and I wanted to cry.

The farther away I got from the famous writer, the more the tears surged in my chest. I couldn't cry here. That would be stupid. This is when my Grammy appeared. "This isn't the end of the world. Pull yourself together. Christ. You're all right."

I walked up to the stage manager, to see where I was in the line-up. She said, "I've been looking for you. You're up after two more speakers. Stay by me."

I sat by her station and waited.

And waited.

She was scurrying around, talking into her radio, crossing things off her clipboard.

When my turn came, the speaker after me—the last speaker—went up. I approached the stage manager, but before I could ask her anything, she said, "We cut you. Sorry."

I was, for the third time in an hour, stunned.

I explained to her that I wasn't going to deliver a speech; I just wanted to get the whole crowd to scream out in anger before they marched. I'd been pumping myself to work up the courage to do this for the past six hours. It wouldn't take more than two minutes to get people screaming their diaphragms out. The whole city would hear it. I explained and explained, and she looked at me and said, "Look, everyone says the same thing. That's why we're off schedule. The march has to happen within a certain time slot."

"Everyone says they're not giving a speech?" I asked incredulously.

"No," she patiently explained. "Everyone says they won't take more than two minutes."

"But I really won't!"

"Anyway, it's too late. The last person is speaking, and it would be disrespectful to her if we let someone go on afterward."

I walked away.

Now the tears would not stay down. My Grammy was trying to soothe me, I could hear her, but after the famous writer shot me down like I was Dick Cheney's quail, there was just no stopping the tears.

Here I was at this huge antiwar rally, surrounded by passive violence: egos, fame, entourages, and a distinct hierarchy over who is and is not important, and *these* are the folks who are opposed to the Bush administration's homicidal machinations?

I decided to leave the rally and forego the march. I could not go on with this total charade. But my Grammy intervened. "You will be gracious," she said. "You were invited to this event, and you will attend it graciously."

I argued with her.

I've had enough.

This is horrible.

I must go.

We went back and forth for a while, my Grammy and me, as I wandered blindly out of the park. I struck a deal. I told her if I walked out and happened to meet up with the march, I would go.

She said, "You're going no matter what."

So it wasn't much of a deal.

I walked down the stairs, out onto the street, and as if my Grammy had choreographed everything, I met the front of the march. Parisha saw me and told me to stand in the front, in the line of famous, important people carrying the huge, Brand Name Antiwar Banner. Hundreds of children were positioned at the very front, so they would be the first ones at the White House gates. This was to symbolize all the innocent Iraqi children that would die. The message was clear: "These are the casualties of bombing."

I thought that was a cool idea.

The march progressed, with the children at the front, the important people carrying the Brand Name Antiwar Banner behind them, and the huge, glorious crush of humanity taking up the rear.

I thought, "Well since we are all following the kids, I s'pose this isn't adhering to a white, male-inspired hierarchy, so that's nice. Maybe things will get better, and I'll see that people are not completely deluded by their own self-interests."

Unfortunately, this fledgling thought was snuffed out like a candle after mass and never had the opportunity to really shine in my mind.

The antiwar officials realized that the CNN cameras could not see their banner because the hundreds of children that they had corralled together *to make a statement to the world* stood in the way. A squadron of officials converged on the children, herding them off to the sides (where there was no room for them), so that the news cameras would have a clear view of the Brand Name Antiwar Banner. Having a recognizable brand, it was explained to me, would bring more people into the peace movement. With the presence of CNN, it became important that all the teevee viewers at home had a recognizable name to connect with peace.

This comes straight out of the Walton family's Wal-Mart playbook.

For the fourth time that morning, I was stunned.

How can you herd hundreds of kids out of the way of a banner during a huge march?

You can't, that's how.

But instead of realizing the pointlessness, not to mention ungraciousness, of this, the antiwar officials and the famous, important people started yelling at the kids to keep out of the way of the banner. The poor kids were in total confusion. They'd try to keep out of the way for a few minutes, but then someone would start leading them in antiwar chants, and they'd get all caught up in the spirit of their songs and naturally ebb out in front of the banner again. Then people would interrupt their chanting and scream at them to get out of the way.

And I do mean scream.

With exasperation, edged with anger.

I was positioned right by the children and saw this abusive, violent behavior happen over and over. Grown people yelling at these kids to honor the space for the Brand Name Antiwar Banner. Some of the kids were visibly distraught. When I stuck up for them, people shot me down, edged away from me, and ignored me for the rest of the march.

So much for the symbolism of death to innocents.

The march wound its way to its destination.

We were barred from walking in front of the White House. important people got arrested, and I walked the long way back to the inn.

When I got there Shawna was out front. I told her the whole story and gave her the copy of my book I'd signed for the famous writer.

Than night, I went back to the Cryptic Lair and played some pool with my buddies from the night before. Again, I felt welcomed and valued. And that's when the grand irony hit me.

Surrounded by activists, feminists, and cultural leaders, I felt uncomfortable and tense.

Surrounded by hardworking men who probably laughed at and told sexist jokes from time to time, I felt perfectly at ease. The antiwar rhetoric of the march's organizers, fixated on a goddamn brand name recognition banner, was simplistic and meaningless when compared to the conversation I had with the Malcolm X Park cop.

And so it came to pass that I found solace from those who are bent on saving the world from the architects of mass homicide, in the company of pool players in a dim, working-class bar and in the complex perspective of a beat cop.

All the way home and beyond, the words and experiences of Arun Gandhi sang in my heart. Passive violence inevitably occurs when people make decisions while being unconscious of their indoctrination.

It is, I have found, pretty much the way of my people.

We are indoctrinated to consider some people more important than others. We allow hierarchies into our lived realities and imaginations. We place fluctuating values on lives. We engage in passive violence even as we protest great violence. Perhaps, worst of all, we completely disrespect children in oh so many ways and fail to serve and protect them as we should because we are busy serving and protecting adult self-interests.

I understood that I had experienced passive violence the whole day of that rally and march. That experience taught me to recognize that when I start thinking I must be crazy, feel repeatedly stunned, and wonder, "Am I the only one seeing the total insanity of this?" then I am almost assuredly in an abusive and passively violent situation. This form of violence is very subtle, and we see it or partake in it pretty much every day of our lives.

It is the American way.

How can we ever hope to bring about positive change in the world when we are so often unwilling to see that we have lived and survived—not at all unscathed—the very indoctrination which *also* manifests in war, abuse, rape, child molestation, hate crimes against humanity, imperialism, and rampant, unchecked racism?

We undermine one another, gossip, manipulate, compare, criticize, and act out within the limited scope of our self-interests.

We do these things all the time, every day.

Say someone—assuredly a bad guy (you are always the good guy)—sets about making your world a miserable place. Then this person takes you aside and says, "You have three weapons: your words, your thoughts, and your actions. I will give you the words to use, provide an environment for your thoughts, and dictate your actions."

You agree to this and set about opposing your adversary with this arsenal they designed.

And no matter how good and nice and peaceful you are, no matter how cagey, imaginative, courageous, and scrappy,

you

will

not

prevail.

As Audre Lorde famously stated, "the master's tools will never dismantle the master's house."

When we are more interested in carousing with important people and putting on a performance that our fellow "progressive" activists will backslap us for, when we unquestionably design and partake in hierarchies, when we believe in "branding," well, we're using the master's tools.

We *become* the master's tools.

How prideful and egotistical we are to think we can change the world without changing ourselves and looking at our indoctrination and *really understanding* where we come from and who we, as a people, are. Humbling ourselves does not come naturally, given our sense of frontier entitlement, but it is only through looking deeply at ourselves that we can ever make a ding in the world's present power dynamic.

Okay now, the people in Bolivia, Iran, Venezuela, Greece, and Turkey—them folks could teach us a thing or two about marches and actions. You don't *ask* officials if you can have a protest and then procure permits. You don't wait around for BfuckenP to fix their holocaust for which they are getting insurance money every single day oil hemorrhages into *our* world. This is *our* world. Us: the manatees, moms, sisters, clams, marsh reeds, herons, dolphins, polar bears, brothers, crows, dandelions, cedar trees, roses, sweet peas, crickets, tomatoes, husbands, wives, harp seals, workers, and beehives. Why are we not storming the Gulf Coast with our cleaning supplies and grim determination? Who do we need permission from to fix some of the horror that we all, as human beings, are singlehandedly responsible for?

Asking questions about permission places you in an inherently weak position.

In Nigeria, where BP has devastated entire regions, people *die* in protests. And the racism of our world has allowed this to happen in Nigeria without all the media hue and cry we see in the white, wealthy US of A.

You ask permission when you wish to respectfully trespass on someone else's time, space, creation, or will. You ask permission if you can swim in the ocean. You ask permission for another cookie from your grandma. You ask permission when you need information that can somehow further your understanding of the deep complexities of life.

You don't ask permission to take to the fucking streets. You take to the streets and you do not leave. People are invariably arrested, injured, even killed when they take to the streets. There is a very strong will that wishes to suck the earth dry and make a tonfuck of money doing so. This power is in command of all law enforcement and military on the planet. So, yes, of course when folks go up against it without tidy permits and tight schedules, this power is threatened and all it knows to do is attack.

This is what happens when people oppose forces such as corporations and/or their government: people die.

Here in the US, many folks lionized Neda Agha-Soltan, who was shot and killed by police during the protests against the fraudulent election in Iran in 2009. The Iranian government has been fighting tooth and nail to keep Ms. Agha-Soltan's family from erecting a memorial because the government knows people will not forget her and will foment insurrection around her unjust death.

There is no Neda Agha-Soltan here in the US. We're all home in bed or at the bar high-fucken'-fivin' each other the moment a protest permit's time has expired.

Don't tell me we aren't a courageous, imaginative, scrappy population. We are. The promise of freedom and independence shapes our personalities and our families, and it doesn't matter if most of it is based on lies or untruths because the spirit lives in our hearts.

And that is a powerful thing.

People fucken' know some things are seriously wrong. But we

haven't chosen our own arsenal of weapons, and so we're organically disinclined to take our own actions. We root through the menu of words, thought models, and actions that are given to us by those who are presently perceived to have more power.

We don't come up with our own vocabulary and thought models, and in the US, I don't think it's a terrible stretch to imagine that people can, indeed, do this.

We come up with great ideas all the time. Community Supported Agriculture is a great idea. It brings farmers and communities together, and most farms are willing to trade labor for food, so it isn't just people who have the cash flow that can get the heirloom tomato and lemon cucumber hook-up. Sliding scale restaurants are a great idea. Legalizing and taxing weed is a great idea.

We come up with different thought models for business, art, science, politics, and education all the time, but when it comes to standing up together and fighting off these bastards who are destroying the planet, we, as a people, get all couch potato.

"We" being all of the people who voted Barack Obama into office and then abandoned him to fix everything for us, and then got mad at him when, without our support, he inevitably got sucked into the corporate power vortex.

We are also the 70 percent of Arizona voters who approved the federal government putting the kibosh on the immigration views of a few perceivably powerful individuals.

There are a lot of us, and we should be taking a much larger part in the present power dynamic.

There's a poem by Shel Silverstein called "Lazy Jane." It is accompanied by his illustration of a little girl lying on her back with her mouth open, who "waits and waits and waits and waits and waits for it to rain."

That's us.

We can do better.

Sí, se puede. That's us.

Chapter 3: **Safety**

It was the middle of the night. Three, maybe four. I sleep deep. Noise and sometimes even touch don't always wake me.

Smells, though.

Smells wake me up.

Once I smelled fire two floors down and called my apartment managers in the dead of night. A woman on the first floor forgot her toast, and evidently her toaster did not pop up or turn off.

Got a free month of rent out of that one.

On this night, I smelled fresh air. If it were August, and I fell asleep with the window open, fresh air wouldn't wake me. This was cold, dark December, though, and my synapses snapped, crackled, and popped to consciousness.

Something was wrong with fresh, cold air.

I opened my eyes and lay in bed for a few moments, felt the absence of Misty Tenderlove curled up next to me. Something was really wrong, and I was scared to find out what it was. I knew I had to get up and see, which was the very, very, very last thing in the whole wide world that I felt like doing.

A frigid whisper laced down the hallway.

It was going to be hypothermic on top of scary.

Shit.

I got up.

The front door was wide open.

I grabbed the phone, hit 91, and let my finger hover over the second 1 as I dead bolted the door. It was difficult to decide whether I should leave the door open in case someone was in the house and I needed to get us out quickly, or if I should hope no one was in the house and lock up. The only thing that was clear was I *had* to find Misty Tenderlove. This anxiety jumbled up my survival skills.

She was in the fetal position on the floor in front of the kitchen sink. Every knife, pair of scissors, and sharp implement we owned was artfully displayed in a 180-degree arc around her small frame.

All the points were facing out, away from her body, a careful symmetrical design.

I love my wife, her attention to detail.

She was sobbing softly, a pool of tears on the floor.

She had been crying for a long time.

Before attempting to get her to bed, I hid all the sharp things.

The knife thing had happened once before, so I hid them real good this time.

The only depiction I've seen of a sexual terrorism flashback in my culture is in the movie *Black Snake Moan*. It is the scene where Rae, Christina Ricci's character, blindly raves through Lazarus's (played by Samuel Jackson) garden in the middle of the night.

Lazarus finds her, and she can't see nor hear him. She's inside a memory, and a sexual terrorist is there in that memory with her. Lazarus leads her back to safety and warmth, but he could have led her to a wood chipper and thrown her in and it would've been the same to her.

When someone is having a flashback, you can't wake them up. They are lodged inside a horrible memory, and they can't get out. That is the problem with flashbacks. They are wily, like coyotes.

To get someone out of it, you have to speak quietly and repetitively. Simple, one- or two-syllable words. "You're safe. You are in a safe place. You are safe. You are safe here in your home. You are safe, safe, safe."

Or at least, that's what I figured out.

Trial and error, like so many things.

Here was the problem with telling Misty Tenderlove she was safe: it was a bald-faced lie and both of us knew it.

Still.

It's a good-sounding thing to say, and it had a *measure* of truth in it, if I was referencing a very specific present moment—though I still did not know if someone had wandered into the house for an easy teevee. I was holding her, the knives were gone, I still had the phone with one button to press in my hand, and both of us were as safe as we could be, for the time being.

In the larger sense, though, she was not safe, not from herself and not from the sexual predator featured in these flashbacks.

I had no assurance that I was either.

For years, long before I met Misty Tenderlove, I referred to the song "Every Breath You Take," by the Police as "the stalker's anthem." Like Nirvana's "Rape Me," I thought it most unfortunate that artists might overlook women's reality in our violent culture and not quite see how their songs could easily be recontextualized by sexual predators. I actually had a lot of respect for Nirvana and was stunned that they came out with that song. I know what it's about, but I could not help imagining some poor kid wandering into the wrong frat house at the wrong time and being gang raped while that song was playing.

You know, for a jokey joke.

The shitstain that Misty Tenderlove came to—quite against her will—know so well did not overlook the opportunity of that song. He was her uncle by marriage. He used "Every Breath You Take" to exert terror and control over her when she was a small child. When the song came out he told her, "Whenever you hear this song, know that I am watching you. Wherever you are, I can see you." So it would come on while she was in the car with him and the rest of her family, and while everyone was having a nice drive, he'd stare at Misty in the rearview mirror, reminding her that her little body was his to do with what he pleased.

It is a very convenient song, like I say, in that way.

It sends Misty into immediate flashbacks. During a flashback, she is transported into a horrifying memory of sexual terror. The present is slashed to bits, and the past jackknives into her consciousness. Any touch, any voice is the shitstain's.

In our daily life, we might be at Jo-Ann's Fabrics or the local co-op when that damn Police song comes on. We must drop everything and get out of there before a flashback hits.

Sometimes we're successful, sometimes we're not.

When we're not, her entire day—sometimes even week—is totaled.

He used rose- or almond-scented lotion on his dick.

Anything rose or almond scented equals flashbacks.

These are, I have learned, common scents in public bathroom soaps. If Misty needs to use a restroom and we're together, I always wash my hands first. If the soap's okay, she uses it. If it's not, she just uses water and a towel.

Artificial cherry and cinnamon come into play somehow. She's managed to block out the cherry and cinnamon memories, but still, forget her ever enjoying a nice piece of cherry pie.

Hammering is another one.

Whenever a neighbor is doing home improvements, Misty tangles with flashbacks. If I need to hammer something, I either wait until she's not home or ask her if she wants to hammer for me. If she is doing the hammering, flashbacks don't happen. She's worked really hard on this one, and lately, I hammer as long as she has a heads-up.

He took the opportunity to terrorize her on almost every holiday get-together. I don't like Thanksgiving and Christmas for my own reasons, so no big loss there, but those are still difficult times every year.

Oh, and the smell of garbage also haunts her, as does the smell of cooking meat.

Since we are both tidy vegetarians, those two don't come up much for us.

This is how we live.

The devil is in the details.

I marvel my ass off, thinking of all the traumatized people in the world, and the things and circumstances that trigger flashbacks. My marriage has inspired me to view people differently and to have more patience and compassion when it seems that someone is being "difficult." A lot of people have a lot of good reasons for seemingly innocuous aversions.

Moreover, though, I trip out on the silent nature of sexual terror. Roughly a quarter of the population, including both adults and children, suffers some form of sexual abuse. That's a fuck of a lot of "silly" secrets designed to keep flashbacks at bay. How many non-veteran PTSD sufferers don't have any resources? How many sexual terror refugees are coping with life the best they can, with little or no understanding from the larger culture?

Banking life on a restraining order.

It boggles the mind when you think about it.

Like many other young people who are sexually abused in our culture, Misty's family did not protect her or keep her safe. In her early teens, after six years of increasing violence and sexual terror, Misty felt very strongly that he was fixing to kill her soon. She intimately knew he was capable of it, so she found the courage and opportunity to go to the police. He was arrested, confessed, and negotiated a lengthy prison sentence. Evidently, though, he "found" that poor man Jesus, so he got out of prison in two years. I really can't see how it would not be devastating for Jesus to see a sadistic pedophile released from prison in His Name. In any case, he was a free man, obsessed with ridding the planet of Misty for "betraying" him by calling the police.

She moved far away. She decided that being a roadie for rock bands was a great idea, so she roadied for much of her twenties.

Eventually she moved all the way across the country and founded the Rock 'n' Roll Camp for Girls. Her idea was to teach girls the self-defense skills and creative empowerment she never had. "Maybe now I am safe," she fantasized. "Maybe I can live somewhere and have a home." She knew he would probably track her down, but the rock camp was too precious and she was tired of running.

After moving from place to place for almost two decades, the Rock Camp gave her a reason to stay put.

It took the shitstain longer than usual to find her, but as soon as her rock camp took off and became famous, he showed up. He made an attempt on her life, but she fought him off. She fought hard because she could not bear the thought of all the rock campers having to cross the place where she was murdered in order to learn how to fight and play music. Like all sexual predators, he is a coward. The moment she fought back and started screaming, he scurried away. He seemed to hold in his mind the time when he had complete control over her life and body.

Maybe it was a happy time in his life.

He tended to show up twice a year, and for a while, we lived on edge.

This was Misty's life until she was almost forty years old, until he was finally jailed for raping someone else.

Until he was incarcerated, we never knew if either of us was safe or not.

It was not a very relaxing way to live.

It is, in fact, terrorism, and a lot of people experience it.

The police were of little assistance. What could they do to protect us against a predator who might show up at some point? We had a panic button in the house for a while, and that was a good thing, but after a couple years, the police needed it back. I designed our home around the availability of blunt instruments. Every room in the house was booby trapped. The men in my family kept telling me to get a gun, but I didn't want a gun. Guns scare me. On the other hand, I feel very comfortable throwing and wielding blunt instruments. A carefully aimed table or lamp is good enough for me.

Misty Tenderlove is a very special person. She is uncommonly compassionate and deeply sensitive to the hurt of others. I believe these traits were borne out of heinous abuse.

Here she is:

One evening we were leaving home in Misty's car. We lived across from a park where a lot of thug-life young men with low-slung pants sold drugs, altercated, and hung out together. As Misty pulled the car around, it was facing a group of kids who sell drugs on the corner. She did not turn on the headlights until we reached the stop sign at the intersection.

I knew why, but I asked her anyway: "Haya, Misty, why'd you wait to turn on the headlights?"

And she goes, "Oh, well, they would have blinded those kids."

Most people could give a fuck about their headlights blinding others, and of those who do, many would not have regarded young corner drug clerks with the same consideration as, say, a family out walking the dog.

But Misty knows what it feels like to be treated like shit, and she doesn't want other folks to ever feel that way.

I wrote a poem about this time before the shitstain finally got carted off to prison.

Where I hope he remains for the rest of his life.

And leaves poor Jesus out of it.

SAFETY

I remember safety.
I remember feeling safe.
I remember crafty safety.
You don't miss it till it's
long, long gone.

Feeling safe and
clean drinking water
have that in common
you know.

It was okay at the time
everyday I would say,
"This is okay, this is okay, today is okay okay okay."
Sometimes I would be crying
when I said this,
but it was still important to say,
like praying is for Muslims n' Christians,
and like chanting is for
Tibetans.
Speaking in tongues, maybe.
Maybe a capella.
I could never tell.
Lord how I missed
crafty safety.
Sleeping well.

Lighting a candle and thinking
about just the light of it
and not the darkness it
casts away.
While
it's
lit.

I never remembered safety
until it was long long gone.

Then I remembered
sly ol' safety.
Crafty, crafty one.
Water, food, air, love,
these are all so obvious.
Safety laughs at
their lack of subtlety.
It is tricky.
Don't let it fool you.
Hold onto it real real tight.
That is, if you got it in your sights.

Healing from sexual abuse takes a long time. Everyone who loves a person who was raped has to find healing too.

Healing requires an enormous amount of time and patience. Most people who have been sexually abused come away from the trauma having learned that they are unworthy of time and patience. It's especially difficult to heal when you're your best hope for healing, and you have been turned against yourself. It's a slow, often lifelong recovery. And I don't even know if "recovery" is the right word. Recovery makes people think "things have gone back to normal," but the whole concept of normal gets shot to shit after dealing with such intense trauma.

There's no normal to go back to anymore.

It's almost like when people have bad accidents or are assaulted and come out of it with such extensive brain damage they gotta learn to read and walk and talk all over again.

When your heart is completely shattered by sexual abuse, you gotta learn how to trust, have sex, and/or love all over again. You maybe hafta learn how to deal with flashbacks and other symptoms of PTSD. But you look fine on the outside, and there's no rehabilitation regimes for you to structure your life around. You gotta keep plugging along, and just like soldiers who return from war and are expected to keep plugging along, a lot of people are just not strong enough to do all this without some serious assistance.

And it's a *fuck* of a lot to do.

Our culture would benefit from looking into this.

Rape, as I say, has been happening for a long time. Been handed down, generation to generation. Families from every possible experience have rape in their past.

We continue to will away this horror show at our children's peril.

Chapter 4: **The Violence of Rape**

In the world there is a priest named Alberto Cutié. Even though he is a cutie, it's pronounced koo-tee-ayy.

In early 2009, someone took photos of him on a Miami beach with his hand down his thirty-five-year-old girlfriend's swimsuit, casually loving-up her butt. The photos weren't published in the media until May—probably because someone wanted to shake him down for cash—but the moment they hit the press, the Catholic Church was outraged.

Outraged, I tell you.

He was barred from the priesthood and shamed by the church.

Quite a response.

Too bad Mr. Cutié wasn't raping an eight-year-old child. Then he would have just been moved to a church seventy-five miles away, and the shame would have been dealt to raped children and their families instead.

But priests never rape children where photographers can see them. They are very careful that way.

Sometime around when this Cutié business was happening, the Catholic Church was hurtled into the maelstrom of another scandal, but their reaction was quite different. According to a report that was almost ten years in the making, over ten thousand children in Ireland had been raped and abused by priests from 1930 to 1990. What's gone on during the past two decades is left to conjecture. Or perhaps we're supposed to believe that priests don't rape and abuse children anymore. The response to this was trying to shut down the report by any means necessary. Not long afterward, outpourings of accusations were made against Catholic priests in Brazil, Belgium, Germany, and a few other places. It seems that anyplace there are Catholics, there are priests raping children.

In a 2006 documentary called *Deliver Us from Evil*, a theological scholar says pedophile priests seek out their psychosexual peers. Living under celibacy, with stunted sexual growth, their peers might very well be two-year-olds.

The film centers on the life and times of former Catholic priest Oliver O'Grady. According to Mr. O'Grady, his older brother began raping him when he was a child. This, he claims, wasn't "so bad" after the two of them started raping their younger sister.

I don't know how Amy Berg, our intrepid filmmaker, managed to get this man to be so candid with her. She is gifted and blessed with an amazing talent. Ms. Berg also got the videotaped depositions of Cardinal Roger Mahoney, along with testimony from O'Grady.

Her interviews with O'Grady, though, that shit is masterpieceful.

Spanning over two decades, O'Grady's career as a pedophile rapist priest began in California in 1973. He raped and/or traumatized hundreds of children and families. He raped a nine-month-old baby. How does a man get his penis into the tiny vagina of a baby? Father Oliver O' Grady evidently found a way. Many parents discovered the abuse and complained to the church. The response was quite unlike the response to Alberto Cutié. The church lied to hundreds of faithful parishioners, lied to investigating law officers, and moved O'Grady from parish to parish throughout California.

For over two fucken' decades this shit went down.

Cardinal Joseph Ratzinger was the head of the office that dealt with sex abuse in 2001 when he sent out an order stating that the church would "handle" all abuse allegations for ten years after a victim has turned eighteen. "Cases of this kind are subject to the pontifical secret," Ratzinger decided. He is also responsible for the policy of moving rapist priests from town to town and stonewalling law officials.

Ratzinger is now the pope and his diligence in covering up the rape of children is coming to the light.

Pope's scramblin' for a foothold.

And I heard Jesus say give him a wee shove.

In summation, when a priest embarks on a potentially healthy relationship with an adult woman, he is immediately banned from the priesthood.

When a priest embarks on an endless series of terrifying and wholly blasphemous sexual assaults on innocent children and the families who trust him to deliver the word of their god, he is allowed to continue his behavior and moved from parish to parish without any warning to those faithful souls who newly welcome him into their lives.

How can anyone be held accountable when *so many* lives are affected by this violence? It is like oil spills. No amount of money can compensate for the loss.

This is rape: moving your shame and bad feelings into someone else's life and body.

I don't know how anyone can truly be held accountable for crimes stemming from feelings that they are completely unwilling to sit down with.

Looking at the facts about child sexual abuse on this planet, it is hard not to come to the conclusion that we don't deal with the epidemic rape of children.

Oh, sure, sure.

When people are *confronted* with the rare commodity of stark evidence, when the rapist lived six houses away and kept our dearly beloved child as a sex slave before burying her alive, sure, sure, we, as a society, get really upset at the man. Usually he's a man. Sometimes it's a child-drugging woman who decides to put our daughter's lifeless body in a suitcase and throw her in the irrigation canal.

The body that came out of our body, the one we gave frozen bites to when it was teething, the one we repaired when it was bleeding, the one we loved and hugged and tickled, delighting in its laughter.

Buried alive, stuffed in a suitcase, tossed in the river after being raped and used like an adult diaper.

Our children, our sacred and beloved children.

How can this be happening? you ask.

Go back, reread the first two chapters, and ponder historical imperative.

Like the Gulf oil hemorrhage, rape is our legacy.

And so what about the cases that don't make it on the ten o'clock news? Multitudes of children are sexually terrorized throughout their childhood. While our culture likes very much to pretend that this does not happen much, sorry, but it does.

A lot.

I can think of many different occasions when adults were sexually inappropriate with me when I was a kid. I happened to have a big mouth and pedophiles generally don't like kids with big mouths, so I managed to get through childhood without anyone raping me.

But the opportunities definitely presented themselves.

One man was my dad's friend, and I remember thinking his eyes were weird and he wanted to sit me on his lap too much. Another man was my uncle Bruce's friend—who did rape a cousin. A female babysitter once wanted me to put ballpoint pens in her pussy. I could not think of one reason I might enjoy this as an afterschool activity and so declined.

I strongly suspect most people's childhoods are littered with similar encounters.

According to Darkness to Light, an organization that keeps statistics on child sex abuse, one in four girls and one in six boys are sexually abused before they turn eighteen. Almost 70 percent of child sex offenders have between one and nine victims; at least 20 percent have ten to forty victims. And an average serial child molester may have as many as four hundred victims in his lifetime.

Of this huge percent of our population that is sexually abused as children, some will go on to terrorize other children, and the cycle of violence continues, gaining momentum, gathering souls. Those who don't terrorize others will, without therapy, turn that terror upon themselves. Addiction, depression, and suicidal tendencies ensue.

The rape of children could be approaching pandemic levels.

Our laws are lax when it comes to rapists and child rapists. Why do these people keep getting out of jail after serving three years for fondling toddlers? Those who fondle toddlers are a danger to society. Dangers to society do not belong in society. Is this rocket science? When a three-striked twenty-four-year-old drug peddler who was saving for college can get put away for life, how exactly does the judicial system define a danger to society?

I have a great idea!

Switch the nonviolent drug offenders' sentences with the rapists' and pedophiles' sentences! Is that too much crazy, impossible dreamin'?

C'mon, now, we allow this to happen. If we did not allow this to happen, pedophiles who had been caught abusing children would serve more time than a teenager caught smoking a blunt.

If we took this issue seriously, pedophiles would, at a minimum, serve life sentences for their first offense.

Instead, they are given three to eight years and time off for good behavior. Pedophiles are very well behaved in childless environments. Then they complain about their lack of rights for having to register as "sex offenders."

One of the present solutions for releasing violent pedophiles and rapists back into society is to keep them in "involuntary civil commitment" after they serve their prison term. Many state and federal facilities have been converted to house pedophiles until they die.

The release rates are very low. Which sounds great, but it costs $200,000 per child rapist per year. Are you fucken' kidding me? The average yearly cost of housing an inmate is $18,000 to $30,000. So taxpayers are footing this exorbitant bill because the sentencing laws against these rapists are not harsh enough. Instead, they live in gorgeous facilities, with hundreds of freedoms and amenities. Because they are considered "patients" instead of "inmates," it costs at least $180,000 more to confine their dangerous asses.

The appellation "sex offender" is, by the way, completely unhelpful. In many states, such as Arkansas, if yer hottie butchie at the women's sex shop refers to a dildo as a "dildo" instead of a "novelty item" to an undercover police officer, s/he will be charged as a "sex offender." Their driver's license will say "sex offender" on it for the rest of her/his life, and their home will appear on maps that warn people of "sex offenders" in their neighborhood. This also happens to people who commit other sex-related "crimes" that have nothing to do with rape, children, or assault of any kind. Lumping all these "sex offenders" together is a great disservice to society. That a sex-shop worker with an errant mouth could be lumped in with people like Oliver O'Grady bespeaks just how seriously impaired the justice system is.

In the case of the "sex offender" Oliver O'Grady, he served a whopping seven years in prison and was then deported back to Ireland, where no one was told of his past. In the documentary, you can *see* him check out a seven-year-old boy in shorts while he strolls through a park. His speech falters slightly, and he cranes his neck as the child passes. None of the Irish folks who share their community with him have any idea of his past, and the Catholic Church has set him up quite nicely with a home, pension, and any other benefit he might need. He is free to rape Irish kids if he wants to. Although *Deliver Us from Evil* has become quite the underground hit and has succeeded in making O'Grady's life somewhat miserable.

So hats off to you for that one, too, Amy Berg.

Unfortunately, there are probably hundreds of thousands of men like Oliver O' Grady living free, happy lives while they leave a trail of rape, trauma, addiction, suicide, and destruction in their wake.

Child abuse is a legacy of our cultural history. This is how violence moves on to new generations and becomes a cycle. Abuse of any kind inspires rage in the victim. Whether that rage is expressed by the later abuse of others, through substance abuse, or some other form of slow-motion suicide depends on the person and their access to help and support.

If the past is not dealt with, the violence will live on.

Usually, the past is not dealt with.

On *Oprah*, parents and kids were talking about the devastating effects of addiction. One family lost their beloved son. When he was thirteen, a coach raped him, and he soon after sought out alcohol and marijuana. As he got older and the psychological terror of rape did not lessen, he needed stronger drugs. Enter coke, heroin, and eventually, death. Enter also the grief of his family who were helpless to save him and could not have protected him from the coach, someone (like a priest) they trusted to have their child's well-being at heart. Child predators are cagey and very good at what they do. The passive violence of winning over parents and caregivers is probably one of the funnest parts for them.

I asked the teevee, "Was the coach arrested for time-lapse murder?"

But the teevee didn't mention the coach again, and there is no such crime as time-lapse murder.

So, no.

A striking number of different artists experienced abuse as children, so it seems that rage from abuse, which destroys a person, can also be turned toward a creative endeavor. Present and historical ranks of celebrities, strippers, directors, visual artists, musicians, writers, singers, models, and movie and teevee stars are positively teeming with people who have channeled the rage of abuse into doing a job very well.

Often while abusing drugs, sex, and/or alcohol.

Folks, this is common.

By the time I was thirty years old and had accumulated a large network of friends, I realized one day that the *vast majority* of them, myself included, had experienced some form of sexual assault in their lives. I am talking men, women, and transfolks, across the board. I know maybe two people who have not dealt with sexual violence in their lives. If you don't know anyone who has been traumatized by rape or sexual violence, either as a child or as an adult, then I will wager that you tend to shy away from deep intimacy with your family and friends.

I think the population, as a whole, is getting sick of rapists. Maybe it's gotten to the point where so many people have been directly or indirectly traumatized by sexual violence, we're hopefully reaching some kind of collective critical mass on this shit.

In a busy Philadelphia neighborhood, a man named Jose Carrasquillo raped an eleven-year-old girl so brutally she had to undergo surgery. The Fraternal Order of Police plastered the neighborhood with photos of the man (he was identified by surveillance footage, tattoos, scratches on his neck, glasses, and other evidence left behind at the scene), along with a $11,500 reward for his apprehension. Within a day or two, he was spotted on the street. A group of neighbors chased him, caught him, and beat him up. The police were called. They arrived and arrested him. They promptly announced that there would be no criminal charges filed against the neighbors because, according to Philadelphia police commissioner Charles Ramsey as quoted by the Associated Press, "These people saw him, he attempted to run and they caught up with him," Ramsey said. "If the injuries had been severe, maybe we'd have to rethink it."

This is a positive sign that people and police are fed up with child rapists.

Still, a quick glance into the blogosphere reveals there is much work to be done. As one pansy-assed denialophile blogger noted:

> We are a society of laws. If we are unsatisfied with the limited jail time that convicted rapists get or if we feel they deserve a much harsher sentence, then we must work with our elected legislators to make the laws tougher. Let's use our system of checks and balances to better ensure a safer society for all of us.
>
> Because no matter how just vigilante justice may be or may seem, it can easily become the first slippery step towards disorder and chaos in our society.

I think it is safe to say that many family members of raped children have considered this option (that is, when the family members are not the ones committing the assaults, then the kid often has to deal with a whole other soulicide of denial) and have worked their asses off to get tougher laws passed. Our system of checks and balances is not working.

Google Amber DuBois to view our system of checks and balances.

Pedophile rapists are never—okay, I'll call it *extremely rarely*—rehabilitated.

No, I mean never.

Once acted upon, the urge to rape children is as undeniable as the urge to breathe. Pedophiles seek out their psychosexual peers. Imagine if someone tried to rehabilitate you from enjoying sex with people your own age. How could this be done? Inside their hearts, pedophiles *know* children to be their own age because their emotional and sexual growth has experienced severe retardation. A fifty-seven-year-old man who has been attracted to eight-year-old-girls all his life is going to be as enthusiastic about rehabilitation as you would be if someone tried to get you to stop having sex with your consenting, adult lover. For the sake of freedom, he might be able to convincingly fake it and *possibly* even refrain from acting on his urges, but *nothing* can stop him from mentally undressing your daughter or son while they are at the public library working on the big geography project with their friends. Pedophiles will *always* be pedophiles. One little slipup means the utter devastation of an innocent child's life.

Meanwhile, most pedophile rapists don't get caught. They are obsessively careful about this. Their lives are painstakingly designed around not getting caught. Unless a child is murdered, the social tendency is to look the other way, to disbelieve, to downplay the slow-motion torture and murder of a child's body and soul. Coach Smith? Never. Dr. Jones? Are you out of your mind? Reverend Bob? That's just crazy talk now. Uncle Bill? Why, I've never heard anything more outrageous in all my life. Even with the reality teevee show *To Catch a Predator* proving this sentiment wrong episode after episode, our own deep desire to deny this atrocity in our midst is often crueler and more devastating to children than the actual trauma itself.

People who prey on children *really* want to be able to continue doing so. They are largely, famously entitled white males who feel it is their right to rape children. They have websites and publications, and swap, produce, and buy pornography. There are no psychosexual peers for them in prison, and so, by nature, they tend to be very, very careful.

Hence the generic neighbor response: "Dang, he was the nicest guy on the block. Always helping out with Little League and taking the kids out for pizza after a big game. Everyone loved him. I just can't believe this."

If a child rapist is caught, but has not killed, his jail sentence is traditionally three to five years. I could get more time for pirating DVDs, as I am reminded each time I rent a movie.

Whenever some kid kills the person raping them, there's always a wiseacre on teevee saying, "Lots of people are abused. They don't resort to murder. This kid should be punished according to the laws of justice."

Yeah, well, lots of people need to eat, but they don't all resort to Big Macs.

Consider Stacey Lannert, released from prison in January 2009, after serving eighteen years for killing her father. He raped her for almost a decade. She communicated this terrorization to a babysitter, guidance counselor, and a shrink in her hometown of St. John, Missouri.

These courageous acts resulted in nothing. No help, no response, no respite from terror, humiliation, and rape.

Stacey's acceleration to critical mass really picked up speed when her father began beating her younger sister. This started when the sister was just about the same age as Stacey when he started raping her. Tom Lannert's psychosexual peer was evidently around the age of nine.

Stacey had fantasized about killing him—often aloud—many times over the years, and one day, she finally snapped.

She shot him, then called the police. When they arrived, she had some weak story about finding him that way when she walked in the door, but the police could tell from one look at her that she had been abused and that she killed him.

Ms. Lannert duly confessed.

During her trial, the jury was not allowed to consider her father's horrifying, nine-year rape campaign against his own child, who also loved him as a dad. This information was withheld. Talk about a mindfuck.

The jury found her guilty, though jurors later expressed anger after finding out about the abuse.

She was sentenced to life without the possibility of parole.

Her lawyers began the arduous appeals process, and she won a right to appeal, but the United States Court of Appeals for the Eighth Circuit ultimately ruled to uphold the original sentence. Here is their reasoning:

> The court rejected Lannert's position that "[a] man who rapes his daughter when she is in the third grade is the initial aggressor, and the author of his own doom." More crucially, the court noted that Battered Spouse Syndrome does not amount to a defense in itself, but merely a support for a claim of self-defense, indicating the frame of mind in which the defendant finds herself at the time of the act. The court declined to override Missouri's rules for jury instruction or interpretation of the Battered Spouse Syndrome law.

Note there is no defense called "Getting Ass-Fucked and Thrown Down the Stairs Every Couple Days by Your Father for Ten Years Until You Fucking Snap Syndrome." And is it not kind of creepy that the only law Ms. Lannert could turn to for help was the Battered Spouse one? She was not his spouse. She was his child. That was part of the *original problem*. He acted out sexually *as if* she were his spouse. This crime against a child and humanity is lumped in with Battered Spouse Syndrome, which is, remember, not a defense, but a factor within a potential defense.

So, according to our system of checks and balances, a man who rapes his child—a person who, up until that point, looked upon him with total love and adoration—is not to be blamed for the actions the child (or anyone) may take in order to stop this terrorization.

If we actively protected children, the poor tykes wouldn't have to go to all the effort of killing someone and then living with that harsh reality hanging over their lives. A child who kills a sexual predator takes on the role of protector for other children, whether consciously or not. Almost always, though, when a kid is compelled to kill an abuser, it's because they want to keep their younger siblings or cousins safe. Children can normalize their own sexual abuse, but to see someone they love subjected to the same abuse provides a serious tipping point.

There is another case currently underway in which a fourteen-year-old named Zach Neagle killed his father. Zach was outgrowing his father's sexuality, and so the man began turning to his younger children. This is when Zach killed him. His crime and defense is similar to Stacey Lannert's. The prosecution is moving forward on murder charges. Our system of checks and balances may very well see this young man serving many years in prison for protecting his younger siblings.

Somewhere out in the world is the man suspected of raping and killing an eight-year-old girl named April Tinsley on Good Friday in 1988.

He has never been caught, but surfaces from time to time and leaves notes for little girls, often on their bikes. In 2004, a five-year-old found a note. Here is what it said in part:

> Hi Honey I Been watching you. I am the same person that kidnapped an Rape an kill Aproil tinsely here is a present foR yo you are my next vitem.

Enclosed with the note, inside a plastic bag, was a condom full of, ostensibly, his jizz.

He must feel very safe and must know that his DNA, if it is indeed his, is not in any database. One wonders how many children he has raped and not killed.

How many.

Recall that the average serial child molester may have as many as four hundred victims in his lifetime.

Let's call that conservative and go with it.

In general, I think we can call pedophile priests serial rapists. They have endless access to children year after year, so let's look there to find some statistics that will inevitably apply to all the other clergy, coaches, health-care workers, and anyone else who consciously designs their life around gaining parental trust and having unfettered access to children.

If you have Internet access, check out the *Deliver Us from Evil* website and click on the Map of Abuse. There you will see red stars on every single state. The states with the most stars have the most

Catholics. Each star represents the number of priests accused of raping children in a specific location. By rolling your mouse over each star, the number of priests accused and the city in which they were accused is revealed.

Let's have some math time.

In Wyoming, the state that seems to fare the best on this map, there are two accused priests in Cheyenne. At most, that would be eight hundred children. In Maine, another state with only one star, 44 priests stand accused. We could call this anything up to 17,600 children. In Illinois, there are 6 stars, adding up to 169 rapists. Multiply this by 400 and you get 67,600. So far, that potentially puts 86,000 kids on the same path as that drug addicted, ultimately deceased young man on Oprah who was raped by his coach. Rape puts kids at a high risk for slow-motion death sentences, after enduring a life filled with debilitating flashbacks, post-traumatic stress disorder, anxiety, shame, and depression with little or no support or assistance from the community. A good percentage of those 85,460 kids in Wyoming, Maine, and Illinois will grow up and rape other kids.

Only with therapy, support, and love do people recover from this kind of childhood terrorization.

Raping a child causes deep harm to *many* people. It divides families, pits people against each other, and renders deep chasms of resentment in relationships. Most often—85 to 90 percent of the time, according to national child welfare statistics—the child knows his/her abuser quite well. The stranger abductions that are blared from our teevee screens make up a very small percentage of child rapes. These are the predators who are chased down by vigilantes.

All the others, the vast majority of predators, we protect and serve.

I love to listen to the newscasters talk about terrorism.

About suicide bombers and mothers who raise their sons to martyr themselves for Allah, for intifada. Meanwhile, millions of children and adults in the world live in terror of terrorists who face only three to five years in prison.

My dictionary offers this definition:

> terrorism | ˈterəˌrizəm
> noun
> • the use of violence and intimidation in the pursuit of political aims.

Terror is defined thusly:

> terror | ˈterər
> noun
> 1. extreme fear: *people fled in terror* | [in sing.] *a terror of darkness.*
> 2. the use of such fear to intimidate people, esp. for political reasons: *weapons of terror.*

Mildred Muhammad lived in terror. Her ex-husband, a trained military sniper, was fixated on her. His name was John Muhammad, and his plan for killing his ex-wife was quite elaborate. In 2002, he decided to snipe off innocent people in the Baltimore area near where she lived, so that when he killed her, it would look like she was just another innocent bystander, and he would then receive custody of their three children. The media called him the DC Sniper, and he killed ten people before he was stopped.

So many kinds of terror in this world.

Being raped brings great trauma into a person's life. While everyone can probably agree that terrorism and trauma are bad things, and while traumatic experiences are pretty common occurrences, our culture phones it in when addressing what terror and trauma—especially sexual trauma—does to a life and body.

If an adult is raped by another adult on a single occasion, it will take many years of grieving to heal. I have spent a good portion of my life contemplating this power equation. Someone can spend thirty minutes of their life brutalizing someone else, and when the thirty minutes is over, the brutalizer is free to move on in life. Having cast off some of his own shame and rage onto someone else's life and body, perhaps the rapist feels quite light on his feet after this half hour. The person who was raped is not free to move on in life. Life, as it was known, has been destroyed and must be rebuilt.

My mother was raped by two men when she was a little girl. This act on that day in postwar London impacted my mother's life so significantly that my siblings and I—born around two decades after the fact—were raised in an environment that centered around our mother's memory. We did not know she had been raped, per se, but the warnings and lectures about safety were over the top. My first book, published almost fifty years after my mother was raped, was an act of divine vengeance—a slight reshifting of the power that was taken from her when she was so small.

I still send her e-mails from people who developed different perspectives on sexual violence at the behest of her experience.

So, yes, one solitary act of sexual terror resonates for generations.

Everyone can pretty much agree that murder is a serious thing—at least when it's not "collateral damage, sorry 'bout that." Murder is willfully ending a human life, and rape is much, much more than the mainstream definition of "forced sexual intercourse." Rape is murdering part or all of someone's soul. Snuffing out someone's power. People often respond to those who have been raped with blame and judgment. Maybe we don't have honor killings here in the US, but we do have passive aggressive character assassinations.

This is very often the case with high school kids who are raped.

Why else would a thirteen-year-old kid in Florida not speak out when four flag football teammates sodomized him with a broom handle and hockey stick in the locker room over ten times in the span of two months? It was already bad enough that the rest of the kids in the locker room saw these attacks and evidently did not care. If he became a snitch, surely the rapes would only get worse. Under this cloud of violence and intimidation, he soldiered on, not realizing the enormity of the crime committed against him or that people would be horrified.

Like any bullied kid, he hoped they would tire of the sport and leave him alone.

This violence will stay with him for the rest of his life.

Unlike the murdered person, the person who is raped keeps living, but their life from that day forward is impacted by the violence someone else decided to visit upon their body.

The terrorism of rape doesn't really ever end. Murder ends for the person who was murdered, but it doesn't end for their family and friends. And it usually doesn't end for the family and friends of the person who did the murdering.

With rape, though, the crime does not end for the actual living, breathing person who has to cope and keep supporting the kids, maybe.

My friend Danica worked for the International Criminal Court in Sudan where gang rape is on par with grocery shopping. Her job was to find witnesses and get testimonies for criminal proceedings. One woman who had the courage to tell her story had been gang raped. Then gasoline was poured into her uterus. Then she was lit on fire. Somehow, she survived.

The actual forced intercourse is the least of this woman's concerns, for she now must live her life with this memory. It will influence every moment of her days until she dies.

I know a woman who was raped by six football players during her first year of high school. Too terrified to go to the police, she was taunted and teased by everyone who knew for the remainder of her high school career.

She managed to stay in school and go on to college—an accomplishment for which she deserves, but will never receive, mass accolades. I met her fifteen years after the football players raped her. This act of violence haunted her and defined her life. She lived in terror that her children might be raped.

Which reminded me of my own mother.

If you are raped in a church, a hospital, or a gardening shed in your grandmother's backyard, it can be challenging for you to enter any of these places—or often, these *kinds* of places—for the rest of your life.

Being sexually terrorized on *one* occasion as an adult is a life-changing experience. Imagine how impacting it is to be raped countless times throughout childhood, as is the experience of hundreds of thousands of members of the population.

If one feels powerless, I suppose terrorizing someone else can temporarily alleviate this.

When a child is presented with a violation for which they have no words, but knows enough to feel shamed; when a child is forcibly stripped of human dignity and respect, often by someone they know and/or love; and when that child is given no resources or even solace, well, I can see how the child can become an adult who feels a sense of power only when they are doing the same stuff to little kids.

It makes sense, and our culture is culpable because in the passive violence of denial, it provides no resources for children who are being, or have been, raped.

Statute of limitations, etc., etc.

Historically, denial is a legacy from when white people—and eventually everyone—learned it best to look away from many different kinds of rape committed against the earth, indians, and black folks.

Schoolyard bullies often feel some sense of powerlessness at home—possibly witnessing their mother getting her ass kicked, possibly being viciously berated for not closing the refrigerator door—and so when presented with a cornucopia of kids who are smaller, gentler, and/or raised in more loving households, powerless children see a place to which they can transfer the terror they experience at home. In this way, like a hearty strain of influenza on the subway, violence moves from person to person. The Internet has ushered the schoolyard into a much more public milieu, and with the imagination that children have, a whole new world of bullying and intimidation has arrived on the scene, causing new kinds of untold havoc.

When humans don't have certain sustenance, they die—either physically or emotionally. Yet so many of us are soldiering on, missing essential pieces of ourselves. We are probably the only animal that can remain biologically living and breathing while our souls are long dead. When that happens, well, that's when we start doing really crappy things like snuffing out our own or someone else's humanity.

There are millions of striations within human civilization's acute disconnect from the world in which we geographically exist. For people locked into their various rectangular distractions, their disconnect can manifest in forms of passive violence—depression and low self-esteem, for example—or compensatory activities such as obsessively acquiring material possessions or "owning" various resources on the planet.

But for those sociopaths who never manage to develop empathy skills and/or who suffer from unresolved trauma or abuse, their disconnect from the world easily manifests in traumatizing and abusing others.

Connecting to nature—including our own nature—does, however, heal much of the sadness and loneliness humankind presently contends with.

For those who commune with nature on a daily basis, who learn to care for the earth and everyone who lives on it, it's hard to see where rape, domination, power, and control actually fit in. There's too much wonderment and too many miracles going on to *actually get to a place* where it might seem like a good idea to rape an eight-year-old.

This is not to say that if we pack up all the rapists and pedophiles and ship them off to get-back-to-nature camp for a few years, they'd rehabilitate. Nor is it to say that people connected to the earth don't also find it in their hearts to rape others.

Once someone has committed themselves to violating another human being—especially a child—on such a grand scale, there is, as I stated before, rarely any turning back. Their humanity, empathy, and connection to the world have been shot to shit. Their soul has died, but their body tarries on.

In Eduardo Galeano's *Memory of Fire*, I learned the white man brought syphilis and rape to Ayiti, now known as Haiti. Not long afterward, he brought syphilis and rape to the Pacific Northwest, as is discussed in Anne Cameron's brilliant telling of history, *Daughters of Copper Woman*. In that book, Granny tells the story of two young girls, aged ten and eleven, who went missing during a Conquistador occupation. The people looked for them all night long but did not find them until dawn:

The first was found face down, floatin' half in and half out of the water, her legs bobbin' in the waves, her eyes open and starin' blind at the sand and rocks on the beach. Her dress was found later. Her body was covered with bruises and bites, her little girl breasts were scratched and chewed, but the sea had washed the blood away. A piece of cloth shoved in her mouth had stoppered her cries and there were blue fingerprint marks on her throat. But what had killed her was havin' the back of her head crushed, maybe by a rock, maybe by the handle of a Keestadore sword. She was dead when they chucked her in the water, but her last hours had been hell and death come as a friend to her.

The people had no way of understandin' what had happened. There'd never been anything like this in all the time since the beginning of life, and so they could only stare at the proof of horror and feel numb shock. They could see what had been done, but they couldn't understand how or why. It had been hard enough to believe the Keestadores would force a grown woman to have sex when she didn't want, but the thought of sex with a child was just too horrible for the people to even imagine, so they didn't know what to think. We didn't let the mothers of the girls near them until we'd washed and fixed them up, and nobody wanted to tell them what the old woman said had happened. Lots of us cried or was sick—or both—just thinkin' of what them babies had been through. Nobody wanted to think about it and nobody who knew could stop thinkin' about it and everybody was . . . was just numb. Just numb.

I figure it's safe to conclude that all the folks between Canada and Ayiti had ample opportunity to discover the white man's favorite historical pastime.

You can look at this and decide I am pointing out yet another shitty thing about the white man, but actually what's more interesting to me is that the indigenous people in both of these locales had no concept of rape before the white man came.

There were no words, experiences, dreams, nightmares, myths, or prayers alluding to rape in the vast and varied worlds of indigenous populations throughout the Western Hemisphere.

Looking at the past two hundred years in the US, people have moved further and further away from nature and their own humanity, meanwhile endlessly replicating the power model of raping indians and the land, and enslaving entire populations of human beings. Rape is intrinsic to slavery; they go hand in hand. You cannot have slavery without rape. Rape is necessary for total control, emotional compliance, and breeding purposes.

Humans rape—each other and/or the earth—to compensate for the isolation in our hearts and the deadened emptiness in our souls. This isolation and deadness comes about through a fundamental disconnect: either rape and murder are always wrong or rape and murder are never wrong. The isolation and emptiness that allows for rape also allows for the violation of everything else that is sacred. You can't have it both ways without creating a disconnect.

And we service our disconnects in so, so many ways.

We are social creatures who are driven to commune with the earth and one another. All kinds of bad things happen when our natural instincts are set asunder by cultural constructs.

Our emotional nature and physical health also take a serious hit from all this corporate hijacking of our humanity. Some of our most basic emotions—fear, grief, anger, jealousy—are generally considered "unacceptable" in our cultural environment. In many holistic healing traditions, a number of diseases—such as cancer—are directly linked to the stress of bottled-up emotions. Strong emotions cannot be contained; no matter what, they will boil over into the world in some negative manner or another.

A century ago, millions of farmers supported themselves and their communities. Which also meant people generally ate seasonal food grown close to home.

Today, unless farms become organic cooperatives and people in the community buy shares, family farming operations are no longer possible.

Companies like Monsanto, Kraft, McDonald's and Nestlé have shafted farmers out of their land in roughly the same manner that settlers shafted the indians. Monsanto—a company whose roots lie in making nylons in Florida—has so rapaciously profited from controlling nature that they now goddishly *patent seeds.*

When Henry Ford and his pals successfully colonized the world's oil for the automobile industry, it was a matter of simple logic that he ventured into Brazil's rainforest to create Fordlandia. Like his forebears, he raped the land and enslaved the indians in order to have a direct supply of rubber for his car tires. No matter that Fordlandia was an abject failure. Ford's sense of entitlement led him to believe he had the right to subjugate certain people to meet his ends.

NAFTA paved the way for companies such as Disney to do the exact same thing to people in Haiti. In order to maintain control of the imaginations of children throughout the world (a fabulous resource), Disney needs to operate factories with the lowest possible conceivable overhead. NAFTA made it so companies don't even have to bother themselves with buying off the local government, which was an olden-time inconvenience to folks like Henry Ford. But believe you-me, when Haiti's president, Jean-Bertrand Aristide told Disney his people have actual human rights, oooh , but there was plenty of the happiest funding on earth to execute a coup against him. He and his family live in exile at present.

Historically, we allowed our humanity to be whittled away because our understanding of reality has been shaped by the very few who have a vested self-interest in maintaining control of the resources on the planet.

During the beginning of the industrial age, creative genius was flowing through the nation like a mighty river. All but a few of these geniuses have been lost in the retelling of history. Those who are still mentioned—mostly George Washington Carver and Eli Whitney—are tokenized. Thomas Edison was one of the founders of General Electric. The corporation eventually stripped him of all power, and perhaps as an exit prize, he was granted a special place in history.

When GE was first formed, it was called Edison General Electric. This partnership proved to be emblematic of all artist/businessman relationships today. GE snagged Thomas Edison's ideas and dumped his name—the infamous wham, bam, thank you ma'am.

Stripping geniuses of all power is another favorite pastime of our culture.

In our violent environment, money and power almost always rape creative genius. And yet without creative genius, there would be no electricity.

At present, the best creative geniuses can hope for is to find a corporation that will sign their paycheck in exchange for the use of their considerable talents.

In the industrial age, a lot of people had an imaginative influx of brilliant ideas. If alive today, George Washington Carver would probably figure out how to run an entire city on the peanut.

Hemp was once a great resource for everything: paper, sail-cloth, work clothes, building materials. But, like Wal-Mart and Home Depot, the cotton and tree men laid down a monopoly on reality. Thomas Jefferson grew hemp, big fucken deal. Over time, hemp has been so successfully stigmatized that today's hemp-growing statesman would be committing some pretty heady career sabotage.

In the early 1900s, electric cars were the vehicle of choice, but like Starbucks, Halliburton, and Microsoft do, the oil, steel, and rubber men laid down a monopoly on reality. Fuel injection is torque, it's power, it's reliability. Death to electric cars. Fast forward less than a hundred years. The exhaust from gas cars is killing the planet. GM thinks that maybe it should develop an electric car and so from 1996 to 1999, they roll the EV1 off their line. But again, the electric car is snuffed out when it makes another successful appearance on the market, in much the same way it was when all cars were first invented at the beginning of the century. Oil people got pissed off and laid down the new reality. None of the electric cars were ever actually *sold*. GM only leased them out. So when the time came to kill the electric car again, they were merely collected by tow trucks when their lease was up, taken out to the desert, and torched.

Yes, as per *Who Killed the Electric Car*, a documentary you should be scurrying to find any minute now, GM and the Bush administration had the entire fleet of EV1s torched in the fucken' desert. That's some serious commitment to oil pals, huh.

If something threatens the financial gain of a very specific demographic, pillage and destruction are understandable and acceptable responses.

That's how we rolled as a frontier nation.

That's how we rolled as an industrial nation.

And that's how we've rolled ever since.

PART II

LOVE

Somehow, in the process of trying to deny that things are always changing, we lose our sense of the sacredness of life. We tend to forget that we are part of the natural scheme of things.

—PEMA CHÖDRÖN

Chapter 5: **Dictionaries**

I'm a writer, so I'm biased.

I can't help but notice that a big part of the reason we are so disconnected from the earth has to do with words. The moment we are born, rather than splash into the great wide ocean, we are thrown, flailing, into a swamped consciousness consisting of our own indoctrinations, unconsidered beliefs, and value judgments.

Before delving deeply into these onerous issues, I'd like to take a moment and talk about the Good Book we rely on for word definitions.

The dictionary is rife with value judgments and unconsidered beliefs and is, therefore, a framework for indoctrination.

I have a complex relationship with words and the dictionary.

On the one hand, my 1965 *Random House Dictionary* is so dearly beloved it almost has its own heartbeat. During my youth, the pages organically opened to "masturbation," "erection," "feces," and other awesome words my siblings and I found hilarious. I cannot imagine my life without that dictionary. It's an item I'd try to save if my house were on fire.

On the other hand, dictionaries, in general, are rife with racism, sexism, homophobia, xenophobia, and other such social pathologies that do not belong in books informing people on the bricks and mortar of thought processes.

Unless you live in a racist, sexist, homophobic, judgmental culture.

Then it is normal and invisible.

Let's look at the definition of "civilization," according to my *Oxford American Dictionary*:

⊚   the stage of human social development and organization that is considered most advanced: *they equated the railroad with progress and civilization.*

Bill Gates's *Encarta World English Dictionary* offers us this definition:

⊚   highly developed society: a society that has a high level of culture and social organization

◎ advanced development of society: an advanced level of development in society that is marked by complex social and political organization, and material, scientific, and artistic progress

And finally, my trusty 1965 *Random House Dictionary* has this to say:

◎ an advanced state of human society, in which a high level of culture, science, industry and government has been reached.

◎ those people or nations that have reached such a state.

Three definitions from three separate sources all provide similar value judgments: "considered most advanced," "highly developed," "high level of culture and social organization," "high level of culture, science, industry and government," and finally, "those people or nations that have reached such a state."

Now value judgments are very, very interesting critters.

Who is doing the "considering?" How is "most advanced" determined? What, exactly, does "highly developed" and "high level" mean? What is the relative gauge against which one might deem a culture, science, industry, or government "high level"? Who are these lofty populations that have "reached" this (magnificent) state of civilization?

It is impossible to consider how influenced we are by our entitled frontier mentality until we start making a habit of always asking ourselves these kinds of questions.

Technological and scientific achievements might make a civilization "most advanced" and "highly developed." Maybe getting people to the moon *is* a great achievement. My personal value judgment on advancements like moon travel is that they're a big-assed waste of time and money that could more wisely and lovingly be invested in the planet we live on. I consider it a most advanced and great achievement for folks to have homes, food, art, music, loving communities, education, environmental synergy, and good health care.

Most every indian tribe in the Americas once provided all of these things as a matter of course. Our current value judgments prevent us from appreciating the brilliance of many indigenous civilizations.

None of this would be a problem if I had found these definitions of "civilization" in "The European-Descended, Male-Identified, Socially Darwinistic, as-Long-as-It-Serves-Me Dictionary." I would say "Great! Now I understand this perspective's definition of civilization!" But I found the definitions in normal English-language dictionaries I have instantaneous access to. These dictionaries' titles *do not give me the information I need.* They lead me to believe I am gaining this word definition from some kind of "general" dictionary, and I am not. A "general" dictionary would take into consideration as many perspectives as humanly possible. This is, after all, *word definition* we're talking about here.

Value judgments have no place in word definitions.

Or rather, *many* value judgments with varying perspectives belong in word definitions.

In this way of thinking, "civilization" would not exclude the following definitions:

- The destruction of your people and their way of life, whose histories date back four thousand years.

- Men with cameras "discovering" your village.

- A constructed reality based on a form of commerce from which an elite cadre of billionaires solely benefit.

- A freeway through your family's farm.

- The absorption of your small town by a sprawling metropolis that was once twenty-five miles away.

- Democracy-bringing that involves carpet bombing innocent people and looting their museums because obviously, since they are being bombed by us, they don't take care of their own five-thousand-year-old treasures and artifacts.

- The death of the last Baiji River Dolphin.

With holistic definitions, one has the opportunity to really ponder the meaning of a word, communicate successfully, and broaden not only one's vocabulary, but also one's worldview. Aren't these, after all, some of the basic functions of words?

The dictionary is important shit, man. It's where people find out what a word *means*. And understanding the meaning of words is the fundamental building block of language comprehension. The dictionary, in short, is where we seek out how to best communicate our thoughts and best understand the thoughts of others. Folks *trust* dictionaries, and yet the value judgments in dictionaries generally involve normalizing some form of male domination or white supremacist racism/imperialism.

My parents were borderline obsessive about us kids knowing the language we spoke. The dictionary was a big part of our childhood. It provided conversation, entertainment, and disciplinary strategy.

We liked to have spelling bees during dinner, and if there was a dispute about a word, someone'd consult the 1965 *Random House Dictionary* in the living room. When we got in trouble for being bad, we'd have to sit at the kitchen table with the parents and dictionary, and recite the definition of our transgression aloud, for example, lie, cheat, dignity, steal, respect, reputation, arson.

A lengthy discussion about the word and our actions followed.

Depending on the severity of our badness, we may or may not have been required to construct sentences demonstrating our knowledge of the word.

Then we would get grounded.

I thought my parents were crazy for creating all this rigmarole about words, but it probably has a lot to do with my own obsessions.

Things get handed down, y'know.

When you're a kid and someone calls you a mean name, sooner or later an older kid or adult will probably arm you with this one: "Sticks and stones may break my bones, but words will never hurt me."

To which I say: "Liar, liar, pants on fire, hangin' from a telephone wire."

Words can, and undoubtedly will, hurt you badly throughout your life. In passive violence, words are the ultimate weapon. The bully knows which ones will humiliate you most deeply, the former friend or lover will abuse earlier intimate trust by gossiping about you and backstabbing you, the coworker will hijack your ideas and use them against you.

If words can be used against you, they can also be used in your service. Your fantastic knowledge of words and their varied, sometimes coded, meanings can greatly assist your smooth passage through the passive violence of our culture.

The power of the passive violence of words—especially coded ones—is something tea-bagger conservatives have learned well. "Family" means white people living in safety with other white people, "values" means interpreting the Bible literally and warping it to serve your self-interests, "elite" means open-minded and educated, and "taking our country back" means somehow getting rid of all the homos and people of color who live in the United States.

It's unhealthy and passively violent to use words like "love" or "war" without ever stopping to define them in your life, from your experience, while taking in as many perspectives as possible.

It is unhealthy and passively violent to rely on our violent corporate environment/culture for all yer learnin'.

To do so renders you an unhealthy and passively violent person.

Words have the capacity to hurt very much, and they often lead to sticks and stones and broken bones later on. Without Karl Rove and Dick Cheney's reptilian mastery of the English language, millions of soldiers, their families, and people in Iraq and Afghanistan would be leading much different lives.

For starters, a lot of them would have lives to lead.

Let's take a look at how today's frontiersman uses words.

Fox News channel's Glenn Beck and Bill O'Reilly fill the airwaves with invective mantras like "Tiller the baby killer" and "mass murderer." Yet when someone does kill late-term abortion doctor George Tiller, these two men take no responsibility. After spending years dehumanizing and objectifying Dr. Tiller, Beck made no mention of his murder the day after it happened. Instead he focused on Abdulhakim Mujahid Muhammad, formerly known as Carlos Leon

Bledsoe, the young black man who converted to Islam and went berserk in an army recruitment center, killing Private William Andrew Long and injuring Private Quinton I. Ezeagwula.

This subject was calculated.

Knowing people would raise a hue and cry about his and O'Reilly's active role, Beck decided to play the "Muslims/terrorists run amok" story because it was part of his rebuttal. If he is responsible for the death of Dr. Tiller, Beck's argument goes, then the "liberal" (another fully unexamined word) media is responsible for the death of Pvt. Long. "The only ones responsible for the death of the recruiters and the death of Tiller," Beck insisted, "are the killers."

A+ on word usage, Mr. Beck.

Good job.

Words are material witnesses to the past, present, and future.

They mutate to accommodate humankind in billions of ways because they—like us—hate getting snuffed on the way to the courthouse. They are our creations and take on lives of their own.

A considered belief is one in which you take the time to sit with something you think you believe. You come to a considered belief after spending time *considering* how other people, with other ideas, experiences, and perspectives, might approach a topic, word, or issue. Considered beliefs are, like words, never stagnant. They mutate and evolve. Taking many ideas into account, considered beliefs are often amended, qualified, or radically changed as time passes.

An unconsidered belief does/is none of these things.

An unconsidered belief is something that enters your mind through cultural osmosis and matches real nice with the blaring voices on the teevee set, so that it seems like fundamental knowledge and indisputable fact.

Unconsidered beliefs parrot what you have been told by someone else, such as your family, teachers, peers, corporatocracy, or the media.

You probably believe in freedom.

What's not to like about freedom?

So what is freedom?

Freedom is many things to many people on this earth.

In Tibet, freedom is living life without interference from the Chinese government. In the US, freedom for Diné (Navajo) and Lakota folks looks very similar to the freedom Tibetans seek. For others in the US, freedom is as described in the Constitution, Bill of Rights, and Declaration of Independence. While generally well written, none of these documents address the freedom concerns of Diné and Lakota people. Here in the US, many people don't factor into the generally accepted concept of freedom at all. And meanwhile, many folks put great store in the fact that this frontier nation of ours is the land of the free.

It will take time to look at what freedom means to even a good portion of these people. You cannot say you believe in freedom if you consider freedom only from your own specific perspective.

That qualifies as an unconsidered belief.

Here are some of the readily available resources for learning what to believe:

The teevee, the Bible, church, the Internet, school, advertisements. Disney, Xboxes, Wal-Mart, GE, McDonald's, Starbucks, Facebook.

Holidays are a good barometer for gauging a given culture's beliefs. The USA isn't really *rich* with holidays and traditions. Not like Iran, Japan, India, or Brazil where people get down with the seasons and celebrate traditions that their grandmother's grandmother's great-great-great grandmother celebrated.

We don't have that here, unless we're native indians, Buddhists, Hindus, Zoroastrians, or Muslims, which most white people are not.

We have manufactured holidays based on unconsidered beliefs.

Corporations have vested interests in all of our traditions and celebrations because our main form of celebration is buying consumer goods for our homes, children, selves, or each other.

Christmas morning isn't exactly Christmas morning until there's a pile of tossed-aside wrapping paper wadded halfway up to the ceiling. During the Christmas holidays in the US, four million tons of wrapping paper and shopping bag waste is generated so we can all celebrate the way we know best.

This is just not how it works in places where they have 4,215-year-old holidays n' shit.

What does it mean when Victoria's Secret sends you one of three hundred million catalogs with the salutation "Merry Christmas" plastered over a pouting, winter-winged angel in her fancy panties?

Well, it doesn't mean, "I love you, your family, and all of your ancestors, and I hope you enjoy this holiday that celebrates our existence in this glorious world."

It means, "Hi, I'm pretty. You or the women you love can be pretty like me if you buy stuff."

That's what we do during our holidays, we buy stuff: fireworks, chocolate candies, roses, green Mylar balloons, US flags, turkeys, ham, birthday cakes, cars, pumpkins, candy, costumes, and champagne.

Wheee!

What we here in the US seem to believe in is buying stuff.

We also have incredibly fucked-up beliefs around food.

It's true that vegetarians and vegans annoy the fuck out of me with their "Meat Is Murder" stickers.

Broccoli goddamn pie is murder.

But vegans and vegetarians tend to be intimate with their food.

People who don't eat animal products are generally curious and involved with their food. Meat eaters in the US pop into the grocery store and buy their savory little white Styrofoam trays with tri-tip, pork loins, or chicken breast cut all pretty and perfect for cookin'. That well-manicured piece of meat in the white Styrofoam tray lounges in the refrigerated section in stark contrast to what the animal went through to arrive on your kitchen counter. How did those animals end up in those rectangles? Well, they died a miserable death after living a holocaust lifestyle. The meat industry poisons the earth and practices some of the most sickening death rituals humankind has dreamed up. Meat workers, deadened to the suffering of those around them, often act out their horror and grief by torturing animals on their march toward death. Those tidy little white Styrofoam rectangles neatly stacked in your grocery store went through hell on earth in order to feed you and your family. Meanwhile, most carnivores would balk at the thought of slaughtering their own pig or wringing a chicken's neck. To most folks in the drive-thru line at Burger King, waiting for their Whoppers while the kids argue in the backseat, the actual killing of an animal for subsistence harkens back to those barbaric times before decency, civilization, and accomplished frontiers were set upon the land.

We are completely removed from the death of our food. I can't think of a more violent, unhealthy eating practice.

My Grammy despised the fact that I don't eat meat. Imagining me living my life without eating meat drove her bonkers. She obsessed about that shit like she was going for Olympic gold. The last time I ate meat was when my Grammy snuffed a rabbit in her yard. She listened to my argument about the meat industry and walked out to the rabbit hutch. She picked one out of his cage, said her good-byes, and chopped his head off with an ax. "There isn't any meat industry in this rabbit," she said, and she set about butchering him and cooking him up. There also weren't any sanitary white Styrofoam rectangles. Just a lot of blood, fur, and gore.

Couldn't fidget my way out of that meal. The poor rabbit still tasted like shit to me, but I do love that Grammy of mine.

It is impossible to avoid developing unconsidered beliefs—and value judgments, which we'll get to in a minute—so don't waste time tryin'.

Indoctrination happens to babies, children, teens, adults.

Pets, farm animals, and hamburgers-to-be also experience indoctrination.

Baboons, wolves, and prairie dogs have indoctrination processes.

The tricky thing about indoctrination is no one really sees it happen, and therefore many do not believe it has indeed happened, especially in a culture, such as the one in the United States, where freedom and individuality are fanatically celebrated by waving flags purchased at Wal-Mart.

The thing here is to recognize your unconsidered beliefs and value judgments, and to consider and modify them as time passes. There are so many of them that you will experience a lifetime of enjoyment uprooting and examining them.

Here is some of the indoctrination I got from my immediate family as a child:

- There is no such thing as not eating meat.

- If you can't swim, you can't possibly experience life, however,

- If you are drowning, remain calm.

- Television is evil.

- Drugs are bad.

- Alcohol is a drug, marijuana is not a drug.

- Doctors, lawyers, the police, and politicians are all, indivisibly, up to no good. It is their nature to be full of shit. Never trust any of them.

- The military is bad.

- You don't have to say the Pledge of Allegiance if you don't feel like it.

- Whatever your Grammy says is what is happening. Never argue with Her.

◎   There are children starving all over the world. If you don't eat
     your dinner, you are committing a crime against them.

◎   It is okay to use cuss words as long as Mom is not around.

◎   Dads teach moms how to cook.

◎   It is *never* okay to lie, cheat, or steal, unless it is artichoke season.
     Poaching artichokes from the fields is not, in fact, *stealing*. It's an
     extended family culinary event, pass the mayonnaise.

◎   It is never okay to eat candy. Have a granola bar or a frozen
     yogurt. Unless it is the morning of a swim meet. Then you can
     eat all the candy you want.

◎   Don't talk while Chick Hearn (Lakers) or Vin Scully
     (Dodgers) is talking.

◎   Libraries and librarians are the pinnacle of any civilization.
     Books are always good, no matter what.

These beliefs and many, many more represent microaspects of
the consciousness in my family. Right or wrong, good or bad, happy
or sad, this was part of my childhood indoctrination from my parents and extended family members.

My peers, schooling, and society in general offered up a further
vast array of unconsidered beliefs.

Some of the family-sourced tenets—such as the evilness of television and the innate goodness of libraries and librarians—I still believe.

Others, such as the impossibility of noncarnivorism and negative attitudes about the military, I have altogether discarded.

It depends on whether or not these beliefs serve the person I am today.

I have worked hard to consider my indoctrination and either build up or tear down various family- and cultural-sourced tenets.

A lot of beliefs come by way of modeling.

Women in my family were generally the ones to hold it down. Therefore, it never *occurred* to me that women are anything other than strong, independent, hard-working, income-producing badasses, who can, meanwhile, sew you a pretty new dress, cook up a damn tasty meal, and delegate your ass into helping out around the house.

When I became an adult, people referred to me as a "feminist" because of this modeling I experienced. But I never really read a lot of books on feminist theory or took women's studies classes.

I've had no formal feminist schooling.

This is important to me because that label negates the idea that maybe a kid can grow up and believe it is *normal* for women to be powerful badasses.

My Aunt Genie taught me how to fish.

My Grammy was Obi-Wan Kenobi and Darth Vader, combined.

My mom supervised a hospital and raised four children. I mean come on. She's a badass. I could never come to any other conclusion about women's roles in society.

No one *said* anything about feminism or woman power in my family. It was a foregone conclusion I came away with.

Westerners often express horror at the indoctrination of Muslim women who wear hijabs, burqas, and abiyas. It is easy enough for westerners to *see* the indoctrination that leads to women cloaking themselves. It is not easy for us to see how we, as a culture, disrespect our bodies, through diets, surgery, drugs, eating processed food, and communing with various rectangles all the livelong day.

My Iraqi friend Iman wears a hijab. She wore it around Misty and me for the first few months that we knew her. When the day came to pass that she did not wear her hijab around us, it really meant a lot. We felt honored and cherished.

Things are always this: complex.

Folks have the *capacity* to see how indoctrination works, at least in other, faraway places like China and Saudi Arabia.

Unless you're Chinese or Saudi.

It seems that it's easy enough to see that *other* people suffer indoctrination. Folks all over the world have the physiological goods to figure out how indoctrination occurs.

In the United States, the land of the free and the home of the brave, where independence and individualism are celebrated, we tend to believe that indoctrination magically does not happen to us at all. Our movies do not affect us. Our television does not shape our worldview. Our parents, peers, religious leaders, and teachers do not mold us into the adults we become.

Here, we have choices.

In Saudi Arabia, "everything is decided for you." In Russia and China, you are "oppressed." In Iran, Iraq, and Palestine you are "a victim of ruthless demagogues and dictators." In France, you hafta talk funny and eat "weird" food like snails.

We don't put much thought into what's decided for us, nor how we are oppressed and victimized by ruthless demagogues. Deep-fried Twinkies is not a "weird" food.

If you go through your whole life without seeing your own indoctrination, then how do you know what *you* actually believe and how do you know the individual that you profess to be?

Teenagers are famous for pissing off their parents and everyone else who comes into contact with them. This is partially due to raging hormones (also why pregnant and menopausal women tend to be touchy), but moreover, because teenagers are at a stage in their human development when they begin to question their indoctrination. Yer average teenager wants to forge their own identity and be respected and validated for the adult they are becoming.

For this, they often rely on their peers—a group of people who are also struggling with the same issues and are therefore of little or no actual assistance.

So a given set of unconsidered beliefs makes a tidy indoctrination.

Value judgments come from unconsidered beliefs. They are very tricky and dangerous. Value judgments allow you to have compassion for some people, but not others. They also compel racism; wildly preposterous, insulting ideas; and other fear-based interactions with the world.

Here is a small example of a value judgment:

I grew up eating Marmite on toast. My mother is Irish, raised in London. Folks in that part of the world enjoy this thickly concentrated, incredibly salty bouillon spread on their toast. It tastes absolutely disgusting to anyone who didn't grow up eating it.

Vegemite, a watered-down version of Marmite found in Australia, sucks.

As an adult, if I don't have Marmite on hand, I'll sometimes enjoy soy sauce and butter on my toast.

Not the same, but reminiscent of Marmite and good in its own right.

Vegemite could *never* substitute for Marmite because it is trying too hard to *be Marmite.*

Soy sauce is not trying to be anything but soy sauce.

Therefore, it is a perfectly acceptable Marmite substitute.

Now, outside of Great Britain and outside of insulting Australians, this passage does not make any sense.

It is a perfectly preposterous microdiscourse brought to you courtesy of value judgments built upon the unconsidered beliefs of my indoctrination.

Were it not for the desire to make a point, I would've been ashamed to write it. It makes perfect sense to me, even though I haven't spent any time *considering* Vegemite. I didn't grow up with it. I tried it once and passed judgment by comparing it to Marmite.

End of my relationship with Vegemite.

Imagine billions of people all over the planet espousing vapid-assed arguments like this.

Which team do you prefer, the Mets or the Yankees? I dunno, but I'll bet someone has not gotten their dream job based solely on the wrong answer to this question.

Which brand of Kim Chee is best? I dunno, but I'll bet someone's grandmother will kick your ass if you dare to bring store-bought Kim Chee into her home. Why is the Old Testament far superior to New Testament? I dunno, but someone certainly does, and that someone might very well be willing to get into a brawl about it with their soon-to-be-ex BFF in a crowded bingo parlor next Saturday night.

These are little indoctrinations. What happens when people get upset about much larger ones?

Well, genocide happens. Ethnic cleansing. Mass rape. Devastation of the earth. Busting into Palestine. Mosques, churches, and temples get bombed. Ancient treasures get ransacked. Salmon, wolves, and polar bears die miserable deaths. Ditto red jungle froggies and the people and ancient treasures of Iraq and Afghanistan. Violence of all kinds goes down, and many living beings, ecosystems, ideas, and sacred things do not get back up again.

Value judgments allow someone to think of something as "wrong" or "evil" based on one's (often incredibly) limited worldview.

Whether you represent the the Oklahoma Sooner class of 1988, Pismo Beach Locals, Sandinistas, Exxon Mobil, the Green Bay Packers, Somali-nationalist pirates, the production team on the fifth floor, Hezbollah, Texas Republicans, the Republic of Tea, or Banana Republic, somewhere along the line you learn a set of very specific cultural value judgments that you may feel incredibly compelled to defend.

This often results in violence—individually, civically, nationally, globally physically, and passively.

And it's time to get on down again.

For many people in the US eating dogs and rats is gross and disgusting. Well, millions of folks in Vietnam think it is gross and disgusting to drink cow milk and not take your shoes off inside the house.

Millions of Muslims and Jews think it is hideously filthy to eat pig.

Ditto millions of Hindus, except replace "hideously filthy" with "ignominiously sacrilegious" and "pig" with "cow."

In fact, by employing an adverb, adjective, and the name of an animal, you can probably account for one, tiny perspective from every culture on the planet.

In the region where I was raised, folks *cannot* have a wedding (or any event, really) without also having a barbeque. The "caterers" arrive with a huge barbeque pit hitched to the back of their pickup, along with many pounds of cow, chicken, and pig. In, say, a wealthy WASP community on the East Coast, if the caterer arrived with a barbeque pit hitched to their pickup, which is filled with meat packed in (invariably Styrofoam) ice chests, there would be some serious-assed bridezilla hell to pay.

My friend Flustarina the Ballerina has a can of beondegi, that is, silkworm pupae, in his pantry. I do not like to view maggoty-looking things. The sight of them really just sickens me, which is probably why I seek them out whenever I happen to be in Flusty's house. We'd have to get into upward of seven digits before I could be paid enough to willingly put silkworm pupae in my mouth and then chew and then swallow and then pick their remains out of my teeth.

Gag.

Flustarina, though, he loves 'em. Mmmm. Gobbles 'em up.

The second I subtract *my experience* from the idea of canned silkworm pupae, I become truly fascinated and filled with wonder.

Like, wow! Through necessity, at one point some folks in Korea ate silkworm pupae. And then in the next generation or so, it became a comfort food and a huge maggot-looking food industry was born.

That is *quite interesting.*

Why, I bet if I look at the food of any given culture, I could trace *all* of the comfort food back to some really hard times for the people, when that was the only food around. How amazing! I think I will reserve some Anthony Bourdain DVDs at the library so I can explore this idea.

Usually, when you have a value judgment and then explore it, you come up with great information that enriches your life and makes the world a better place. So, hee-haw, right? I mean, how can this be a problem? Why cling to your unconsidered beliefs and value judgments when it's really just a buncha fun tearing them down?

Crazy diamond, crazy diamond, tear that shit down.

It is my job to think about words and what they mean, and about dictionaries and what they say. Words are how I get along in the world. Words are my job.

It is not a high school student's job to think about this dictionary shit. It is most people's job to learn a definition of a word, gain an understanding of it, and employ it in their vocabulary, if necessary.

So part of my job as a word nerd is to point out that our dictionaries compel us to accept many things about the world that actually *impair* our ability to broaden our perspective. In every book

I write, I bitch and moan about the dictionary, and I spout my embarrassing fantasies about making a dictionary someday.

I dream about it all the time. I would call it "The General Dictionary." It would take teams of thousands to canvas the earth. Each word would take up at least a page. Each letter, a five-inch volume. God, it would be grand.

My perspective is—like any dictionary writer's—limited. Some of my beliefs are considered, some are products of my indoctrination. It is my fervent hope that readers will come away from this book with a desire to ask difficult questions of themselves and the world, and moreover, to seek out answers that may or may not fit within the schema of their present consciousness.

In this spirit, I offer you the cover of this book, which my friends Bob and Mariko designed.

There, you will find 101 words. Bob, Mariko, Misty Tenderlove, and I spent a few days coming up with a list of over six hundred unexamined, taken-for-granted words. From there, Bob printed up the words in the order we thought of them, cut them out into pieces of paper the size of fortune-cookie fortunes, and secured them, still in order, with a rubber band. Our Bob, he is very orderly.

Then came the evening of elimination rounds. It was brutal at times, and we all (well, I) cried to see certain words leave the list. In the first round of elimination, we put all the related words together. This left us with roughly half, and dang Bob could fit only a hundred (I insisted on 101) on the cover. So we discussed each remaining word and voted and voted and voted on them. We all picked a "personal best" and agreed "izzat" must be the last word.

It is our intention that you spend a good portion of your time defining—through dictionaries, discussions, life experiences, and engagement with others—all of the words on the cover.

Though it may take quite some time to holistically define each of the words, this exercise will, I guarantee you, rip you out of your culture/environment and place you sweetly into the world.

Have fun with that like the world depends on it.

Chapter 6: **You Are Here**

Here's another ocean story for you.

This one time when I was around eight, my dad, older brother, and me all went on a trip to Baja California in our yellow and green Volkswagen van. We camped at lots of beaches and had a great time. Somewhere down by Loreto, we went for a walk on the beach. It was a rocky one, and I left my sandals in the van, so I walked in the water. My shod brother and dad soon outpaced me. It was a beautiful day, the sky was blue, the ocean sparkling, and a light breeze tickled my skin in the sun. No one else was around. I walked along in the water and then, midstep, my right leg wouldn't go down. It was frozen in place, bent at the knee, ready to hit the water for, you know, the next step. I stood there on one foot, perplexed. Then I tried to push my leg down with my hands, pushing with all my might. It would not budge. I'd never heard of this happening to anyone, and to this day, I still haven't. Finally out of ideas, I looked into the water. There, right under my frozen, hovering foot, was a gigantic stingray.

I screamed.

It fluttered away.

My leg went down, and my dad was running to me. He got there in time to see the stingray. I tried to tell him about my leg freezing, but I was too freaked out to make myself clear.

I obsessed about this for the rest of the trip, and the memory is pristine. It blew my mind.

What kept my leg from stepping down?

My friends talked about god and some went to church, but no one talked about god grabbing their leg to keep them from getting stung. Stingray stings hurt like hell but are rarely fatal. They're really peaceful folks, and I felt bad for scaring it when I screamed. My frozen leg probably wasn't a miraculous life-saving intervention.

It was just fucken' weird.

I saw very clearly that the world was quite alive. Furthermore, the world *must* be aware of me. I *must belong* in it, like pie and caribou and ferocious hurricanes.

Some *force* froze my leg and saved me from a lot of pain.

Freak out!

Was it god? A guardian angel? Nuestra virgen? Was it some vortexish magnetic energy? I never have known, but I did learn that I am a tiny part of something much, much larger, and sometimes larger things make themselves known in truly wondrous ways.

Aside from a de rigueur miserable, self-absorbed stint as a teenager, I have been thankful ever since.

In Thomas Berry's essay "The Spirituality of the Earth," he writes:

> There is a certain triviality in any spiritual discipline that does not experience itself as supported by the spiritual as well as the physical dynamics of the entire cosmic-earth process. A spirituality is a mode of being in which not only the divine and the human commune with each other, but we discover ourselves in the universe and the universe discovers itself in us.

I think I was really dang lucky to discover myself in the universe at such a young age. Lotsa folks go from the cradle to the grave without seeing themselves in the universe. Hence Rush Limbaugh.

It's one of the disconnects individual and collective members of humanity face. We and the world around us are raped and murdered as a result.

I gotta say, though, I love that Father Berry is a Catholic. This shows that it's not *impossible* to connect a given religious doctrine to actual lived reality.

Which includes the world. And the universe.

Reverend Cecil Williams of Glide Memorial United Methodist Church in San Francisco is also really good at connecting people with themselves and the world around them. I love to attend his services, where homos, elderly Japanese folks, hookers, junkies, black and white folks, children, celebrities, politicians, homeless folks, undocumented workers, hip-hop stars, and people in wheelchairs all crowd in to feel close to the divine.

Generally, divine things are big and make your heart sing.

I had a divine experience in an earthquake, where the force of the earth rushed into my heart and tore through my bloodstream and apartment in 4.2 seconds. It did suck that so much of my home and community were torn apart, but I, personally, was high as a kite on a *very happy* adrenaline rush for two weeks afterward. Bearing witness to the earth's power filled me with laughter, joy, and inexplicable hope.

Probably, it's one of those rooting-for-the-underdog things.

"The divine," in Glide Memorial's case, is everyone being together; listening to words that come from a very fiery, kindhearted man; and taking in the joyous music of the Glide Ensemble.

Maybe Jesus is there too.

I would *so* be there if I were Jesus.

Glide Memorial honors his life and teachings by *being* his life and teachings. It does what a church is *supposed* to do if a church is all about atoning for the fact that Jesus died in such a fucked-up way. Glide takes in the homeless, feeds people three meals a day, has a drug rehabilitation program, offers HIV/AIDS testing, and provides many other free services to the community.

Even yoga and meditation!

It's located in the Tenderloin, which is one of the most difficult places on earth to gentrify, bless its heart.

Reverend Williams took the crucifix down in the 1960s because he said it is a symbol of death, and his church is all about living and life.

Fuck, yes, Reverend.

As far as I can tell, various religions serve humanity by giving us a point of reference. Through various teachings, religion helps people understand our place in the world. Sometimes miracles are involved, but often religion seems to provide mundane encounters with the divine, which is always comforting, especially when the chips are down.

I discerned this as an adult, for in my home life as a child, I never heard a good thing about religion.

"Religion" generally meant various sects organized around Christianity. There were few Hindus, Muslims, Sikhs, Jews, or Buddhists in Santa Maria, California, home of Hiking Viking Chevrolet.

Saturday night sleepovers at friends' houses meant a royal Sunday afternoon pain in my ass. Most of my friends went to church, which meant if I wanted a kickass after-church breakfast—possibly even in a restaurant, depending on the family—and more fun time with my friend, I had to go achurchin' too. When I got home, my father always seemed to have the time in his life to be waiting for me at the kitchen table.

He'd "invite" me to sit down, which was really just psychological warfare because there was no escape. So I'd sit down, and he'd grill me about every last detail of the sermon (of which I usually remembered nothing) and my general church experience: "What did the preacher say? What songs did you sing? Do you think you're a sinner now? You are *not* a sinner. What did you learn about god?" This is a person with an audio- and photographic memory who terrorized religious solicitors with verbatim passages from the Bible. He seemed to expect me to remember things like he could, and it was difficult to make him understand that I *totally* tuned out during church services. I studied hats and faces and stained-glass windows, all the while fantasizing about the possibility of blueberry waffles with whipped cream at Pappy's. I understand now that my father was probably scared that his child would "get" religion, but he needn't have worried. I was bored to tears in my friend's churches.

The catholic priest droned on and on, and I thought I would die. The only part that seemed remotely entertaining was getting the holy communion, but I was never allowed to partake in this because I did not have a holy communion with the lord, and I knew my father would never allow me to spend the night with my Catholic friends if I expressed any interest in getting holy communion with the lord just so I could actually get off the pew and have the experience of some priest sticking a wafer in my mouth.

So even that minor diversion was out for me.

The fundamentalist Christian church made all the kids go to Sunday school. The teacher got everyone to recite various prayers and psalms that I did not know. If you could recite the prayer or psalm, the teacher gave you a piece of sugarless candy that tasted like shit. I knew this because I memorized the prayer or psalm as it was recited by other kids in the class. Again, the lonely minor diversion.

The only church that was fun was the Baptist church. There was rousing music; women stomping around, having total fits in the aisles; and everyone joyously singing. They even had an electric guitar, bass, drums, and a preacher who shouted instead of monotoning me to numbdom come. Still, it was entirely unclear what message I was supposed to take away. He screamed about burning in hell for eternity, and I could not figure out how this preacher had any idea about what I'd be doing for eternity. He didn't know what I did yesterday and he didn't know what I'd be doing tomorrow, so how could he have any insight on my eternity? Made no sense, and wasn't a gripping enough mystery to try and figure out.

My father's actions were equally mystifying. I did not care about, ergo, understand a thing that the various religious leaders were saying, and I really, really didn't understand why it was so important for my father to take the time to inundate me with questions every time I went achurchin'.

Heaven, hell, salvation, damnation.

Who gives a rat's ass when there are trees to climb and roofs to jump off of?

I mean, really.

Harmony Glover and Riz Rollins, two of my most treasured friends, helped me to understand Christianity. Many other folks I have met along the way have taken the time to teach me about Islam, Hinduism, Judaism, and Buddhism.

Harmony Glover was an elderly woman I befriended when I was going to school in Olympia. I used to go out to her farm and hang out with her. She was deeply into Christianity and loved Jesus with all of her heart. At first, I tuned her out when she talked about Jesus, until she told me this story:

One day during World War II, her mother was very sick. At this time, gas was rationed, so people always drove to town together for trips to the grocery store and whatnot. On this morning, Harmony's mother asked her to go to town and get some food with a neighbor man. For some reason Harmony could not quite explain, she was afraid of this man. She felt a deep sense of dread as she walked through the forest to the neighbor's house. She became so frightened that she recited the Lord's Prayer out loud while she walked. She asked Jesus to stay with her and to guide her. By the time she got to the neighbor's house, she felt a sense of calmness. And when he pulled a gun on her and told her to take off her clothes, she felt Jesus standing beside her. She paid no attention to what the man was telling her to do and instead recited the Lord's Prayer out loud, alternately insisting that the man put the gun down.

Eventually he did.

Harmony was convinced that Jesus disarmed the man. She left his house, tore through the forest, and told her mother what the man did. He never came around her or her family again.

As Harmony told me this story, I swear to god, there was a light shining through her.

She glowed.

It blew my mind.

I felt the spirit of Jesus for the first time in my life, and suddenly I understood—not the droning on and on in the Catholic Church and not the reciting of psalms for shitty sugarless candies in the fundamentalist church—but I understood that god could indeed be found in a church. This possibility had never occurred to me before, although I did, upon reflection, recognize this spirit in the women having fits in the aisle of the Baptist Church.

In one afternoon, I realized that my father was wrong about religion. Not wrong about organized religion in general, but essentially wrong about how awesome and great Jesus's love is. Anyone who could help a child survive a sexual assault is a-okay in my book.

I allowed Jesus into my heart on that day, and He has never left it.

Mostly, I feel deep sadness for Jesus because of all the horrible things done in his name, but he tells me that love and light happen for everyone in their own time, in their own way.

I can't say that I see it, but I do believe Jesus does.

I am *positively thrilled* that I did not have a religious upbringing. Thank you, thank you, thank you, Mom and Dad, I kiss your feet on that one.

Outside the tenet that anything with a spark of life inside of it is god, I have never been wedded to any particular idea about who god is. I am quite free to be open about any and all religions. If a religion has some ideas I find inspiring or that make sense to me, I adopt them. My home, also known as my church, is filled with icons and beliefs from many religions. I've never squandered my time and energy on god's good earth by feeling guilty, thinking about whether or not I am sinning, or making up for the fact that good ol' Jesus got nailed to that cross. I know what a sin is. A sin is lying, cheating, or stealing. There are no other sins. I know these to be sins not because of my family indoctrination, but because god and karma always cut my ass down *immediately* after I commit any of them.

When I offer up anecdotes about my childhood, my friend Riz Rollins sometimes laughs and says, "Inga you were raised by wolves." This is in general reference to my being brought up by hippies at the nudie beach vis à vis Riz's memories of growing up in the South Side of Chicago.

My dad and Uncle Bruce mostly offered up the wolf factor, but Grammy and my mom were of a similar mind, sans the nudity.

Uncle Bruce would smoke a joint, track down a few kids, and make us sit there with him and watch the tide come in or go out. *Seriously*, we'd sit there, and he'd point out every speck of minutiae that evidenced the tide's activity. "See there now, see Bird Turd Island out there? Ten minutes ago you couldn't see as much of it as you do now. Can you see that? Keep watching." As children, the siblings, cousins, and me were bored to sobbing tears, but if you didn't sit with him and pay attention, you'd get scolded about not giving a shit about how beautiful and amazing the ocean is, and believe me, the boredom was better than the scolding of a stoned, naked hippie, obsessed with us kids paying attention to the world.

Then there were the tide pools. Uncle Bruce knew the name of every plant and animal that lived in the tide pools, and we kids were expected to know their names, what they liked to eat, why the tide pools are the perfect place for them, and what a teeming, miraculous, wondrous place tide pools are.

"I mean, my god, do you realize all the shit that's going down in this here tide pool every second of every day? Watch it. C'mere now, *I don't care* if you want some raisins. You can eat in a minute. Get yer ass over here and plop down and watch these sea anemones dancing."

I think the stoned hippies thought us kids were all stoned too, but then it is kinda true that kids are pretty much high all the time.

For flower arrangement day at school, we weren't allowed to buy flowers, oh, no. All the *other* kids might have fabulous, sparkling lilies and glorious, pink roses enshrouded with baby's breath from the store, but *Joe Muscio's* kids lived in *a world filled with flowers!* Flower arrangement day was an opportunity for our dad to lug us out on a Sunday drive hunting down wildflowers, and we of course had to know the names of all of them.

For show-and-tell, we weren't allowed to bring in toys or games. Our dad's idea of show-and-tell was spending an afternoon catching tarantulas sunning themselves on the hot pavement of remote country roads. We'd get to keep them for a week and take them to school before putting them back *precisely* where we found them.

We weren't allowed to be afraid of animals. To express fear of boa constrictors; huge, slimy, flopping trout; warty bullfrogs; grunting pigs; or psychotic geese was the Christian equivalent to saying "fuck you" to the lord.

Camping with the hippies was another good time. It involved hiking for hours with a backpack crammed with all your stuff; chopping wood; catching, gutting, and cooking fish; picking berries (which may sound quaint enough, but we had to know the name of the berries along with the names of all the critters who depended on them for sustenance); hefting water; cooking on an open fire; and taking baths in the river or ocean, where we weren't allowed to use soap unless we had the Expensive Biodegradable Camping Soap. When we didn't have the soap, we hunted and gathered smooth flat rocks to scrub our butts with.

It wasn't until I was a grown-up that I saw the point of any of this.

But, yeah, raised by wolves.

That's me.

This upbringing was weird and influenced by weed, but it blessed me with teachings about my place in the world. I did not need church or a spiritual figurehead. I had the world to explore and the oft-naked, unrelenting hippies to preach to me. My dad and Uncle Bruce were simply the loudest and most aggressive teachers, but Grammy, Aunt Genie, and my mom were always haranguing me about nature as well. I was *never free* from learning experiences, lore, and consciousness of the natural world.

I have met so many people who have no connection to our earth and this world, and they are always just the loneliest folks to meet. I have never felt this kind of loneliness because there is always the wind to visit with or some ants to stare at.

My loneliness resides in the world man has made. I feel like a fucken' alien dinosaur most of the time. I don't have a cell phone unless I am traveling. I tried to have one but found that people expected me to be available all the fucken' time. People would *get pissed* at me if I didn't call them back right away. With a landline, this doesn't happen. So good-bye cell phone.

I am a Luddite when it comes to present technology. It pulls me deeper and deeper into the world man has made—a world I have been at odds with my entire life. Why would I dive into Facebook or the iPhone when my yard needs weeding? I haven't visited the goats and chickens all week, and the kids down the block have a blackberry lemonade stand going on. I spend enough time on the phone and e-mail. I don't need to commune via technology that much. I like other folks in this world as well.

Our culture could literally transform overnight if we all of a sudden woke up one morning and placed enormous value on the life going on all around us. If we magically, collectively understood that there is a place for us in the world and the world desperately needs us to love it, things would change lickety-assed split. This would bring about a massive self-esteem uplift, and doing shitty things, or standing by while others do shitty things, would no longer be tolerable.

I am in awe at how complex and impossible this transformation presently is.

It is such a simple thing, and it seems so possible.

Chapter 7: **Defending the Home Front**

One of my favorite words is "izzat." It is a noun and means the regard in which you hold yourself.

Izzat is important.

People have the capacity to do really shitty things to others and ourselves when we do not tend to our izzat. In our violent culture, it's your izzat that keeps you from going down and taking others with you. When you know you are worth loving and fighting for, then you can love and fight for the world. Protecting your izzat is the most basic form of self-defense.

People think self-defense is learning how to knee someone in the balls. Under the right circumstances, that could be one miniscule aspect of self-defense. Knowing how to physically protect yourself is not, in and of itself, self-defense.

Real self-defense has more to do with izzat.

In self-defense, you are a sacred being on the planet and you have every right to take your place in the world. Self defense is knowing your place and communing with your environment, while having compassion for and respecting other folk's place. Self-defense is making firm boundaries with those who wish to take you from where you know you belong. Sometimes self-defense is pleasant— a warm smile and a firm shake of the head. Sometimes it requires one to break through the boundaries of what is considered acceptable behavior. For women and girly men, this is not always an easy thing to do. We are often taught that being attractive involves being pleasant and polite. Firmly asserting your place can easily involve being disagreeable or rude.

In every self-defense class I've ever taken, it is always terrifying and shocking to see so many women do not know how to loudly and assertively say, "NO!" Many of my classmates, especially ladies born in the 1950s, had a very difficult time raising their voices at all.

I have saved myself from bad situations many times by raising my voice and being disagreeable or rude.

At a party in high school, everyone left the room I was in at the same moment. I was looking at records and didn't realize I was left alone with a man, until I felt a bad feeling. I looked up from the records to see why I had a bad feeling, and then I saw the man. He came closer to me, with a smile on his face. I did not like this man and did not want to interact with him and had no idea why. I was hunched down at the records. If he got close enough, he would be standing above me, and I would have been trapped at dick level. I stood up before he got close enough and immediately left the room.

Very rude, but self-defense nonetheless. I listened to the feeling in my body, sought out the source for it, assessed my physical situation, and took immediate action.

I would rather be rude, paranoid, mean, bitchy, and disagreeable than raped.

Months later, I heard he liked to drop roofies in girls' drinks and take them home for a night of happiness for himself.

Where is that man now? How many women did he drug and rape? Will he ever see the inside of a prison cell?

When I was around twenty-one, a friend, Jojo, and I went on a road trip from Olympia, Washington, to California. One night we were on Route 101 right by Salinas. I was dozing in the passenger seat when Jojo, in a panic, woke me up. "That car is following us," she said. "They won't leave me alone." I looked to my right, and a car with two men in it was right alongside us. I could not see them well. They were white. They could have been in their twenties or forties. They dropped behind when my head popped up, and I thought they figured Jojo was alone and would leave us alone when they saw she wasn't. But they passed us and slowed down, then dropped behind us again, staying right on us.

I saw a sign for the Highway Patrol and told Jojo to take the next exit. We followed the signs, but horror-movie unfortunately, they led us to a dark and lonely two-lane road. The car was still behind us. We decided to pull up to a house whose lights were on, hoping the men would think we were going home and someone would be there to help us. The car passed the house, and we waited in the driveway for a little bit. Thinking we'd outsmarted them, we pulled back onto the lonely road and started driving back toward town. I kept looking behind us and saw no car. After a few minutes, though, lights flooded our car. The men were suddenly right behind us again. They'd been following us with their headlights off the whole time. I was shocked that I hadn't seen them at all. We freaked out, but were near the town and pulled into a busy gas station. Jojo stayed in the car, to see if their car pulled in, and I ran into the store, filled with customers. I breathlessly told the clerk to call the police and recounted what had been happening.

As I spoke, a man walked into the store and grabbed a Hawaiian Punch out of the refrigerator. He listened to me talk. My body clenched up as I watched him, and even though I didn't get a good look at either of the men while they were bothering us, I knew with all of my heart that this was one of them.

I don't know how I knew, but I knew.

So I looked directly at him and said, "Why are you and your friend bothering us? What do you want? What's your plan?"

Everyone in the store stared at him, and the clerk pulled out a large baseball bat. The man dropped his Hawaiian Punch on the counter and ran out of the store. The clerk followed him with the bat and took down the license plate number of the car as it raced off. They'd pulled up behind the store, and Jojo hadn't seen them. The clerk called the police. When they showed up, we told them everything that had happened. They told us to wait at the gas station while they tracked down the car. After fifteen minutes or so, the police came and said they found the car and would hold the men to give us time to get back on the road. They said they couldn't arrest the men as they didn't break any laws.

These two men enacted an elaborate predator/prey scenario because they knew they were free to act with impunity. Most predators are mindful that they can keep things in a "she said/he said" context. How many women and young girls will they terrorize before either of them sees the inside of a jail cell?

Seriously, the power equation here is badly fucked up.

I thought a lot about that night I recognized a bad man I had never really seen before. If I hadn't recognized him when he walked in the store, I don't know what would have ended up happening that night. They seemed very determined to continue stalking their prey. I knew he was one of the men because I was tuned in to my surroundings and to the feelings in my body. I seized up when he walked in the store. My adrenaline surged through my body at the sight of him. I watched him get the Hawaiian Punch, smiling and happy, and there was no question in my mind. He'd followed me into the store to hear what I was saying, to revel in my terror. But he froze on the spot when I outed him in front of everyone, before running out of the store.

Cowardly shitstain had the nerve to terrorize two unarmed young women, but couldn't face being held to account for his actions.

From this experience, I really, really learned the value of listening to my body. His *presence* set off a physical reaction inside of me, and that's fucken' powerful. The only reason my body would react like that was if it sensed danger that the social conditioning of my mind might have otherwise rationalized away. It was scary to run into the store and tell everyone what those men were doing. What if no one believed me? It was scary outing him in front of everyone. What if I was wrong? But we were in *danger*, and my body, present in the world, shut my mind down. None of my actions that night were rational. I was driven purely by animal instincts, and my instincts served me well.

I learned to watch out for police station signs soon after I got my driver's license. One of my favorite things to do was drive to the ocean late at night and sit there in my car, writing. One setback to this activity was it attracted predators, many of whom followed me in their cars. The first time it happened, I was terrified. But it didn't take long to realize my action was attracting a hidden population of people, generally men. I quickly learned to memorize license plates through the rearview mirror and drive around until I found a cop, hospital, or police or fire station. One dumbass followed me right into a fire station parking lot. I laid on my horn, and he was trying to turn around when the firemen came running out.

He got away, but still, that was a good time.

If I wanted to be a teenage girl writing by the ocean at night, I had to adapt to my environment. And my environment has bred sexual predators since slavery times. The *safest* thing to do would have been to stop writing at the beach at night, but it was just too beautiful to give up. Instead, I developed a survival strategy for doing an unsafe thing.

Another time in a nightclub, someone in a crowded passage grabbed my pussy. And I don't mean just above it or off to one side, I mean full on, my goods in their hand. It was far too crowded to see which person it was, and my body took over. With both my hands, it grabbed the offending wrist and would not let go. It used all of my body weight to drag the person, causing the crowd to part, horrified. And it stomped the man on the floor until doormen pulled me off. The idea at first was to kick me out, but my boyfriend or someone intervened. I was allowed to stay and the pussy-grabber was ejected.

Oh, joy, justice.

How unique.

I remember this vividly, and it still feels like an out-of-body experience. Not to diminish the violence of my response or anything. What I did was violent and brutal, I totally own that. If I could do it over again, I wouldn't have stomped him more than once. My response was an action equivalent in animal energy to his energy, which compelled him to grab my personal goods. Had he not cast that energy toward me, I certainly would not have sent it back at him.

In all of these situations, the me that generally muddles through the world on a daily basis was replaced by an animal hell-bent on survival. I don't have any serious fight training. I've studied self-defense and pay attention to martial art moves and stuff like that, but I am not a disciplined fighter. I'm not a badass, but badassedness has always been interesting to me and therefore in my consciousness. Like I mentioned earlier, I read *The Art of War* pretty regularly. Other than that, I don't know where all these moves and strategies come from. My body finds openings and moments in the world to defend itself. If I can give my social conditioning up to the lord and allow the world to guide and protect me, then I can have a hand in shaping my destiny.

There are many moments like this in life—not all of them have to do with dangers—that are very powerful, life-changing experiences. The more we pay attention to them, the more auspicious and tuned-in our lives become.

Know your bad feelings and trust them.

If your skin is crawling, pay attention. If something doesn't feel right, pay attention. If the hairs on the back of your neck prickle, if your gut clenches up, if a wave of wrongness washes over you, if your heart starts beating faster, pay, pay, pay attention. Do not second-guess yourself or rationalize anything that impedes your safety. Our instincts are the animal inside of our humanness, warning us of danger. Most animals have better instincts than we do, so pay attention to animals too.

I have seen the grunion run, when the ocean turns silver with fish for as far as the eye can see. If you stand in the water, a perfect, oh, maybe six-inch circle of sand appears around your feet. The grunion feel your energy and avoid coming into contact with it. You can literally *see* the actual space you take up in the sand, outlined by glistening silver for miles and miles. If you get a friend to lie down in the shallow water, you can see the entire space a body occupies. It is a very beautiful and life-changing sight.

The grunion showed me that. Thanks, grunion.

The selfish, cranky goats in my backyard teach me joy, the art of war, and wiliness. They aren't my goats, but belong to the school behind my house. The school also has chickens, which hang out in my backyard and the neighbor's too, along with the goats. The goats are mean, and they have rectangular pupils—another rare occasion where nature produces rectangles. I was pretty much not very interested in them one way or the other until they both escaped into the front yard. I chased, and they dodged and ducked, feinted left and dashed right. Finally, I caught one of them by the collar. I started pulling him toward the gate, and do you know what that goat did? He did something that made me fall madly in love with all goats, forever. *He ran in the direction I was pulling him,* causing me to stumble and let go of his collar. What fucken' genius! Who are these brilliant animals? How is it I have not really noticed goats before? I love the goats! It took me a half hour and the bother of two innocent bystanders to get them in the backyard again. After that I warmed up to them, and they warmed up to me. It fills my heart with happiness when I holler "Goats!" out the window, and they come ascamperin' and ableatin' up the hill and into my yard. They bring me laughter, and I am always in awe of their total insubordination and intelligence.

And they let the chickens ride on their backs, so they're willing to give the underdog a leg up.

This crazy world has the most interesting folks in it.

Noticing all this kinda stuff is how you learn to be present.

Izzat soars when you are present in the world. It is very good feeling to know that the world needs you. And when you are part of the world, defending it is another form of self-defense.

In Hawaiian, there is a word, "kuleana." It means both privilege and responsibility. Hawaiians know it is a huge privilege to live in such a beautiful place, and with that privilege comes the responsibility to fight developers, protect beaches and fragile coral reefs, educate kids about how awesome the world is, or pick up the plastic that global currents send to Hawaii's shores.

I learned that word in a documentary called *Hawaii: Message in the Waves*. It featured people who understand kuleana and design their lives around the responsibility of their privilege in many different ways. One is a teacher who gets kids rowing out in the open ocean, teaching them the importance of teamwork and relying on each other. He also teaches them the power of, and respect for, nature. Another is a surfer girl who picks up trash on Hawaii's northwest islands, which have served as a resting place for millions of tons of plastic since the 1950s. Some help tourists understand that the coral reefs are so delicate that merely touching them can set things horribly off balance. All of these people have a vitality about them, a sparkle in their eyes; they are sun kissed and fit. They are angry and very sad, but mostly they let their kuleana guide them into positive actions.

That's what I've noticed about all people who are present in the world—whether they're farmers, nurses, businesspeople, bakers, musicians, taxi drivers, or artists. It doesn't matter if they know the word or not, kuleana guides their positive actions, and they glow from within.

I once made up a game to help me remember to be connected to the earth and the world, even when I am far removed from nature. It is a very boring, slow, and monotonous urban game that can only be played while walking. I love it! You can play it by yourself or with others for points. It's called "Somebody Put That There," and it goes like this:

You look at everything you can possibly look at and as soon as possible, say either "Somebody put that there" or "Somebody did NOT put that there." "Somebody" being a human being. Look at parking meters, doors, trash in the gutter, pigeons and crows, cars, trees, parks, fences, gardens, restaurants—everything in your vision. It is really a skill to find something where you get to say "Somebody did NOT put that there." Here are some things that somebody did NOT put there: a fallen leaf on a car windshield, a tree root erupting through the pavement, a look of wonder on a toddler's face as she stares down a big red dog, most birds and other critters—but it can be argued that most city- and town-dwelling fauna would not live there without the presence of humans putting things like fast-food wrappers, muffin crumbs, and trash cans all around.

By playing this game, I developed the skill of connecting with my world, no matter where I am. It's part of my izzat maintenance and keeps me aware of the things going on that do not have to do with social constructs and the corporate environment.

When you open yourself up to the world, the world will give you the opportunity to protect yourself. Learn to fight with you mind, with your consciousness, with your body and invite the world in.

There are many other aspects to self-defense that do not involve an external predator. Some of the things that can make us unsafe live inside our own hearts, as has been exhaustively discussed throughout this book. Here's a few ways to defend our hearts:

Spend time:

That dumb movie *Buffalo 66* changed my life in an oddly fundamental kinda way. Vincent Gallo plays Billy Brown and Christina Ricci is Layla. Billy just got out of prison, and he kidnaps Layla—who doesn't have a last name, which exemplifies the total lack of imagination that went into her character. The movie is about Billy Brown, and like so many movies and lived realities, Billy is the only one who matters.

Still and all, he's a compelling character, who's always talking about "spending time." You know, just spending time together, having moments of closeness and good talks. I disliked a lot of things about this movie, but the "spending time" thing gave me a good term for something I strongly believe in.

Just spending time with friends, family, or strangers.

Let's spend time.

Wheee.

Sometimes people are far away, but you can still spend time through phone calls, cards, or presents.

Spending time is investing in humanity. Take the time to let people cross the street or move safely in front of you into your lane. Hold the elevator doors, tell the bus driver to stop when you see someone booking it right as the bus begins to pull away. Let the person who only has a couple of items go ahead of you in the grocery line. If someone is a bit short at the grocery store, cough up the $2.25 instead of allowing them to experience the humiliation of giving some of their food items up. Pay the toll for the person behind you before crossing the bridge. All of these things take a few extra moments of your life, and they enrich your own sense of self and humanity. Spending time is a daily practice that defends your heart against the mean-spiritedness of our culture/environment.

Practice Anger Meditations:

I once worked at this restaurant, and on my first day, the cook, Tom, took me aside and showed me a window that opened to an empty space between buildings. It wasn't an alley, for there was no entrance or exit, just a brick and concrete space that architects and time had forgotten. The window was a couple floors up from the ground, and on that ground was a carpet of glass and plate shards. Tom handed me a plate and said, "See, you can get really stressed working here, and almost every day someone will piss you off. If you get really mad, come on in here to the kitchen, grab a plate, and throw it down as hard as you can."

I did not know at the time that Tom was giving me a gift I would hold dear for the rest of my life, but it sounded like a damn fine plan at that moment. I immediately smashed the plate he'd handed to me, and we both smiled with warm satisfaction. If I ever get the chance to thank him for that one, it might involve feet washing.

I keep saying anger because anger is related to grief, depression, loneliness, frustration, resentment, helplessness, and most other shitty feelings, so I'm *saying* anger, but I'm *talking* about all the normal shitty feelings that come along with this being-alive racket.

We don't learn to release anger in a healthy way, and when we hold anger in, we attract bad vibrations and energy.

As kids, when we have fits—if we have fits—the general goal is to calm us down as soon as possible. My parents did not have this system. They thought that kids have feelings and kicking the wall for twenty minutes while screaming at the top of your lungs is certainly an expression of feelings. I was allowed to have fits because anger is normal. Maybe they noticed I was a nicer kid for a while after I had a good fit, I dunno. Neither of my brothers had fits, but my sister did.

In any case, this plate thing along with the memory of having fits when the world was just bringing me the fuck down helped me to deal with my anger as an adult. I was really deeply horrified when I realized that it is wrong to express anger when you are a grown-up. See, but *anger* isn't a problem. Anger is actually a great force and can lead to serious creative and emotional breakthroughs. The trick is to *not communicate with others* when you are angry, to recognize when you're angry (never a problem for me, but a lot of people are so uncomfortable with their anger, it is quite difficult to diagnose), and to act out your anger in a conscious manner.

The bathtub is a good place. You can go under the water and scream yourself blue and no one can hear you. Cars with the stereo blaring are also good for this, but only while stopped in traffic or at a light.

Don't scream and drive.

If you can find a place where it's safe to break glasses and plates, oh, but you are a blessed soul. When I lived in San Francisco, I found a place by a subway vent that was kinda like that empty space at the restaurant, and I'd go to Goodwill and buy ten plates for a dollar and get all kindsa hurlin' mad with them.

This was a weekly practice for a period of time when I wrote my first book.

Slamming doors is also very satisfying, but again, not while engaging with others. I mean just standing there and slamming a door for twenty minutes.

Another one I like to do requires a large, open space. I take off my shoes and throw them as far as I can, screaming as I release the shoe. Then I run up to wherever they landed and do it again and again until I am tired and need a cup of tea.

Great, great, exhilarating fun.

This one, though, is best if you do it with a few friends because then it looks like some weird thing a bunch of people are doing in the park instead of just one crazy person who might get the cops called on them.

When you're having your fit, keep focused on what you are upset about. Verbalize as much as you can, even if it's just a haggard guttural groan. This gets all that badness out of your body and into the universe, which is big enough to deal with it.

I know all the peaceful people love to think that anger vibrations are harmful to the universe, but if the universe can handle the starving cries of human, polar bear, and frog baby populations, well, it can handle my being pissed off about so-and-so backstabbing me like a twelve-year-old jackass. The universe can handle the anger and destruction vibrations of forest fires, earthquakes, and tsunamis. It can handle people getting pissed off to live and love better lives.

Anger meditations are just as important as relaxing and having a nice time. In everyday life, anger, resentment, and frustration are bound to build up. Maybe not *all* the time, but *over* time. Even if you are a peace-loving yoga person, you still suffer from life's disappointments. When left unchecked, negative emotions generally roil over into passive violence toward yourself and/or others, which makes the world a shittier place, and you, just another misery maker living in denial. Defend yourself by allowing your anger to come out in healthy, considered ways.

I like to do various anger meditations a few times a year just to clear my head and body of all my shitty emotions. This really helps me in my writing, and it helps me to be a better friend, lover, and family member.

Get pissed off in a good way and allow your anger to serve you.

You can't change the world, but you can make it a better place. You can be healthy, loving, compassionate, and sensitive to the needs and feelings of others. You can have daily life practices that bring small happinesses. You can do your best to consciously live without perpetuating violence. You can bring comfort and love to the people around you. You can listen and hold yourself accountable. You can trace your unconsidered beliefs and value judgments and figure out if they really serve the person you are today. You can learn when and how to fight. And you can protect your izzat and other people's too.

If you think of yourself as a plant, all of these things make you strong and help you to thrive. When you're a plant, you can't do anything about storms, freezes, and blights. All you can do is make yourself strong so that in the event that you are suddenly at the mercy of something bigger than you, well, hopefully the strength you have cultivated in yourself and your life is enough to see you through.

All this has a lot to do with love, and the dictionary kind.

There are many important loves in this life. There is the love between friends. Sexual love should never usurp friend love. But there are lots of other loves around us, some we may or may not see. Your neighbors benefit from your love. Nothing's stopping you from cooking up a double recipe of lasagna and taking it over to one of your neighbors once in a while. The kids running around the neighborhood sure could use a bowl of that watermelon you just cut up, leaving plenty for you and your family. Perfect strangers enjoy your love when you help them load their groceries in the rain, when you let them ahead of you into your lane, when you stop for them so they can cross the street. Lordisa, the birds, squirrels, raccoons, deer, and bees love you when you hook them up with sustenance. People bitch about raccoons, but did you know they love cat and dog food? A big bag of cheap pet food will keep the raccoons out of your space and away from your pets better than any gun or trap. In love, though, that's not the motivation for feeding them. In love, you feed the raccoons because you honestly want the best for them.

Call all of this karmic investment, if you wish. This still traces back to selfish motivations, but if you think of loving the people and the world around you as a way of protecting yourself against things that are bigger than you, it would suffice. I like to think of loving the world as putting into and out of myself exact reflections of the world I want to live in.

And it makes me happy to know that the hummingbirds and crows are fed and that the kids are laughing with watermelon juice running down their sticky faces and arms.

There are so many much bigger realities that bring pain and anger that I've learned to seek out small joys every day. It is one of the greatest forms of self-defense that I know.

My friend Bob enjoys collecting Japanese stickers, as do I. He is more frugal than I am and, unlike me, will not buy them when money's tight. Whenever I have the disposable income to buy myself two sheets, I send him one in the mail, even though we live in the same city. I do not enclose a note or anything. Just the stickers. Bob does not thank me more than to let me know that he got them and that they made him very happy.

He also knows not to reciprocate. He knows it brings me joy to send him stickers once in a while. I like to imagine him coming home from work to an envelope. He will force himself not to open it until after he has washed up and eaten dinner. The anticipation will give him a thrilling surge of adrenaline. When he opens it, he will giggle like a kindergartener and will set the stickers somewhere so he can view them for a day or two before he places them in his sticker box. I like that this minidrama is taking place across town. It is a simple thing that brings joy.

If Bob reciprocated, it would detract from the pure joy of giving.

He finds other means of giving me gifts.

We have never discussed any of this because we both love the world very much.

And that's what our friend self-defense is all about.

Chapter 8: **My Mother's Roses**

We've talked a lot about violence.

Now let's talk a smidge about love.

Love is good mutater.

The meaning of "love" changes throughout life. It does not mean nowadays what it meant when I was in fifth grade. It takes a lot of self-examination and life experience to see the full capacity of love. One of the key hallmarks of real love—which our culture fails to identify for the most part—is a commitment to adore the asshole that someone is. To fully protect and revere someone's weaknesses, phobias, insecurities, and maddening habits, *as much as* their glowing qualities. It is easy to love how great someone is. It is difficult to love what an asshole someone is.

And make no mistake, everyone is an asshole.

If you think you are not an asshole, then that is one of the most assholish things about you, right off the bat.

Me, for instance, I am a claustrophobic basket case with social anxiety. I am prone to outbursts of anger, which usually stand in for frustration or helplessness. I am cranky when I'm too hot and bitchy when I am too cold. I often hurt people's feelings with direct statements that are unnecessarily candid, and I mispronounce words a lot.

I suck!

So do you.

Wheee!

In nature, I have noticed, there aren't many rectangles. You can find them in crystals under microscopes, but unless you look really, really hard, nature doesn't produce much in the way of rectangles.

In contrast, the people of "civilization" can't function unless they're doing it inside a rectangle, holding a rectangle, and/or staring deeply into the maw of a rectangular screen.

Rectangles—that is, our obsession with creating them and our growing dependence on them—are a mass manifestation of our disconnect from nature and the world.

This teevee-, computer-, and iPhone-induced fugue-like disconnect must be maintained or we may discover real intimacy with the world around us and with one another.

If your goal is to achieve these things, you've got to think about love differently than you are used to.

Real love means finding value in most everything, and new ways to value yourself, the planet, animals, trees, people you like, people you don't like, and so on.

In love, you do not care if your child does "well" in a sporting match. You care simply that your child is having the experience of sporting.

In love, you do not consider someone "marriage material" based on their income.

In love, you do not bury your emotions so deeply that others become fodder for your deepest fears. Therefore, you do not start a whisper campaign about the nice-looking woman in your office who rebuffed your sexual advances, or because you are jealous of her appearance.

In love, our aging parents are our elders to whom we owe a great deal. You do not stick them in an old-folks farm, unless they express a desire to live in such a place.

If we are a culture that loves, none of our children would be "banned" from the family because they are homos, or because they chose someone outside the family's race or religion, or because they are transgender.

In love, you bolster and support, you do not try to "change" anyone.

You can change the violence of our world sooner than you can change an individual.

Many people who choose not to partake in the violence of our environment—but don't teach themselves to give and receive love—end up offing themselves.

I've contemplated suicide many, many times.

But when I sit down with myself, I gotta admit that suicide counts as violence, not love. It makes no sense to commit an act of violence because I can't hack the violence around me.

Dang, that's out.

So instead, I've cobbled together a way to love in the world.

Every fall my mother cuts her roses back.

Another way of looking at this is: she ventures out into her garden with her clippers and ruthlessly wallops off the branches that provided her with literally hundreds of roses over the last six to eight months.

Oh, dear god, when I was little, I cried.

To see my sweet, caring mother orchestrating this massacre seemed like a betrayal. I threw fits and begged her not to carry out these unspeakable acts of torture against her otherwise treasured and beloved rosebushes. Was it only a matter of time before she turned on my siblings and me with the clippers?

"Look," she'd say, sweaty and annoyed. "In order for the flowers to happen, the branches have to be cut. This is how the bush rests and gathers strength for a new year of blooming."

Crying, inconsolable, I'd retort, "Why *do you* have to decide how it rests?"

"Inga, there won't be any flowers next year if I don't do this."

How could my mother be so cruel and callous?

Our *dad* was an asshole who yelled at us and made a big ruckus. If *he* had been the one who "cut back"—a.k.a., decimated—the roses, it wouldn't have been nearly as horrible.

It was a baffling mystery until I was ten or so and finally caught on to the rhythm of the roses. My mother's roses grow lush, so much so that you get all heady in their presence. Then it starts getting cold, and they get all brown, with rose hips filled with nutrients. When the rose hips die, Mom lops off the branches, and they are ugly all winter long—ashy and gnarled, mean and nasty.

A winter rose bush is one of nature's most frightfully ugly creations. Unearthed, it could be a medieval weapon. If it's old enough and if someone were to fall in agreement with certain laws of physics, a winter rose bush could impale a person.

The green and red, pink, or yellow beautiful, grooving, blooming orgasmathon from three short months ago is unthinkable. If the winter's real bad, you can maybe completely forget what all that graceful graciousness looked like before.

But then, we have here every spring when them little green nubs start in, and soon, the spectacle of untold beauty explodes. Gently obliterating what looked like artfully arranged dried, spiky colons for the past few months.

In order for the roses to dazzle your days, painful acts must go down and really bad ugliness has to be the reality for a time.

That's the rhythm of roses.

It is also the rhythm of sex and love and child rearing.

And the balance of life.

And many other things.

This is the garden where I learned that bad things and good things are part of each other, and there's shitall you can do about it. Cry, bitch, moan, manipulate, or claw your way to the top, nothing will change the fact that things will totally suck in your life, consistently, from time to time.

The best course of action, I have found, is to face and accept bad things, and not try to make them *seem* good.

Also known as giving it up to the lord.

By the time I was a teenager, I'd cut back her roses for her.

When my brother Nick passed away, Grammy bought sixteen rose bushes, one for every year of his life.

My mom put her grief and love into those roses.

They are quite beautiful. They stay alive on your kitchen counter for two or three weeks after you cut them.

If she ever moves to a different house, the roses go with her.

Love is a verb.

Love is something you *do*.

It's not something other people bring into your life.

Many people are looking for love in all the wrong places.

A five-minute perusal of personal ads looking for love on any website will either consciously or unconsciously address any or all of the following questions:

What am I gonna get out of this?

What kind of financial, sexual, and/or emotional security will I gain?

Are you physically attractive enough to make my friends envious?

How will my self-image improve if I sleep with/commit to you?

Will my esteem in the family rise or fall if I bring you home for the holidays?

This is not any way to go about "getting" love.

Love's a manner of being present in the world, not a perfect set of circumstances that leads to untold happiness for you, your lover, and your life.

You can't control love, and if you try, bad things will happen.

Some things are bigger than you and love is one of them.

I think the misconceptions surrounding this simple tenet are at the root of many abject failings of humankind. It is the reason the mineshaft collapses, the reason the wildfires tear through newly constructed housing developments, the reason there is no water and our food supply is poisoned, the reason the earthquakes are quakin', the reason there exist terms such as "dead zone" and "fished out," the reason coyotes eat the family poodle. People just can't face the fact that some things are bigger than them. If we mess with things that are bigger than us, bad things will happen.

The oil holocausts in Nigeria and the Gulf of Mexico, for instance.

As I described earlier, humans failing to comprehend that some things are bigger than them is the reason for all of this and much, much more.

When something is bigger than you, it's always best to relax and comport yourself in a respectful manner. It is not best to suck it dry and/or make the most money you can off of it.

The language of violence that we grow up to see as normal provides us with a totally useless definition of love.

To propagate this useless definition, children are told The Story. It goes like this:

You are a kid now, but one day you will be a grown-up. You will fall in love, get married, and have children of your own. If you are good at being a grown-up, you will have a college education, a rewarding job, a mortgage, and car payments. You will really, really, really care about sex, romance, religion, sex, romance, fashion, and/or NBA championship games.

The Story is meaningless to a child. It is impossible to conceptualize being a grown-up. "Having" children is inconceivable—no pun intended—when you're a kid. Even when you're a kid who is raped, impregnated, and bears a child.

I had the kind of parents who think it is best to let their kids know where babies come from. The thought of my father putting his goods inside of my mother's body utterly nauseated me. I could not *believe* they had done such a thing enough times to have four children.

Ewww.

Nonetheless, The Story is also profoundly impactful. Therefore, it's important to understand why it is told. Regardless of whether or not parents are truthful about how babies are made, The Story is repeated in so many different ways by so many different adults that it heavily influences the parameters of every child's cultural identity. As every grown-up knows but could evidently give a fuck about, parameters cause a lot of problems when the realities that shape your cultural identity and *who you actually are* do not seam up nicely.

Which, by and large, is what almost always ends up happening to most grown-ups at some point. Which is why, for instance, male federal judges and stockbrokers wear frilly panties under their bespoke tailored suits.

Living an endless series of lies is a form of violence.

Hence, Wellbutrin, road rage, suicide and divorce rates, the booming porn industry, and the prevalence of sexual violence.

Among other things.

It is only a story, but it makes you feel real bad when you don't measure up, and most folks don't measure up.

For example, some kids are homos. The whole "marriage and kids" story can get really depressing after a while and often leads to suicide. Since homos can't get married, you know this big-assed annoying story does not apply to you if you are a homo.

Some kids aren't sure if this life they keep hearing about is the life for them. Maybe marriage sounds like a bad idea. Maybe having kids and a mortgage is not attractive.

Some kids are artists, musicians, or writers, and they know there is no money there because almost everyone in their lives will discourage them from believing they can make a living according to their talent, often referencing someplace called "the real world."

Some kids have talents that are not considered appropriate for their race, religion, ethnicity, or gender.

Gordon Ramsay is one of the richest chefs in the world.

His father told him that being a chef was "poncey." You know, pretentious and kinda faggy. So Gordon, he sets about becoming the richest, most hypersexually masculine chef on the planet, but his father didn't live to see it, so having no peace on this, our Gordon becomes a caricature of himself, a macho commodity destined to create a corporate empire.

He's a winner! Look, Dad!

He's won!

He's rich and famous, and his beautiful wife is referred to as a "limpet" in the UK press because he is so *not* poncey that he is known to assert his masculinity via other women.

This is called overcompensating, and it happens to a lot of wealthy "winner" people.

So these things are important, these stories people tell kids, these lessons children learn and the culturally imposed experiences they have while they are growing up.

In aboriginal culture in what is now called Australia, when children are born, people watch them closely to see what their natural talent is. When everyone discovers what a child's natural talent is, the family and community do everything in their power to nurture and bolster the child's talent.

Or at least, for many people, that was the common practice before the white man and his frontier-nation mentality came to their land, and in just a couple hundred years, ruined a place that had been quite lovely for thousands and thousands of years prior.

What if we were a culture that encouraged everyone to do according to their natural talent? What would such a culture look like? Isn't that what the whole idea of America was in the first place?

Natural talent is *bigger* than your desire to be successful in playing out the stories you are told as a child. You aren't gonna *feel* right if you are living in subdivision hell, in over your head with crazy payments, if all along you've wanted to be a trapeze artist in the circus.

Same for the love in your life.

But the thing of discovering what a child's natural talent is—that seems like a good practice to me. Imagine all the unhappy people with stifled dreams who could be happy people with realized dreams.

La, la, la.

Love, American style, goes something like this:

You meet someone.

The two of you come together.

If this is a one-night stand, you have sex—possibly quite wonderful, spontaneous, passionate sex—and you never see each other again. Or, if you do see one another, maybe you will have sex again, and maybe you will feel uncomfortable and awkward, and maybe you will pretend you don't see each other. When the awkwardness happens, it's generally because you allowed someone you don't know to partake in the most intimate biological act you are capable of, and it feels weird to have shared this part of yourself with a total stranger.

If this is a love affair, you will maybe do a li'l courting before you have sex, maybe not. Your whole experience will revolve around maintaining the honeymoon period. Neither of you can do any wrong, the sun rises and sets upon your heads, you have wonderful sex, your heart pounds when you hear each other's voice.

All is bliss, the rosebush is in full orgasmic bloom.

Some people can carry on love affairs for decades—especially when they are extramarital. Some love affairs last a couple weeks. It all depends on how long the two of you can maintain a reality based on illusory bliss.

Then the actual relationship begins. The length of time this lasts also varies fantastically, but it can result in marriage and the whole until-death-do-you-part thing.

Sex, usually sooner than later, also happens. There is the honeymoon period. Oh, dear god, no one has ever loved in this way in all the history of humankind.

Blah, blah, blah.

Then come the times when you begin to notice that your lover's cute little idiosyncrasies are, in fact, annoying as fuckall. Possibly, your lover is even abusive and controlling. But you remember the sighs after sex, the warm times, the hot times, and you decide that these idiosyncrasies are bearable.

You learn to ignore them or negotiate them in other ways.

But then, eventually and inevitably, the shit hits the fan. The real complexities of human nature seep into the honeymoon bliss. This is when the "problems" start in a relationship. Unless you are willing to accept your own failings and those of your partner, these "problems" will end in separation and/or divorce.

Sometimes everything sucks, and there is nothing beautiful in the world, and that is the truth. It's awfully important to keep in mind during these times that the *focus* is to learn and grow and to have good times even while bad times are happening.

Good feelings and times are just as natural and easy to come by as the bad ones. Of course, this is complex, and what is bad is not always obviously bad until after you experience the badness for a while and say, "Man, I feel like shit." Who knows how long that might take? Prisons are filled with women who killed their lover or spouse after twenty-five years of serious rape and/or ass-kickin'.

So you can't always feel those heady love vibrations. This shit is fleeting and *grows* into really deep affection. I don't know why we are taught that love is some kinda wonderful thing. It is *such* a lie. Sometimes you and love are ugly and gnarled up, and you are probably hurting pretty badly.

Most cultures and families don't offer this teaching.

After the thrill is gone, after the honeymoon is over, *that's* when the rosebush gets lopped off. Pining for that honeymoon time dishonors all that is to come, but generally, folks get stuck in that feeling of wanting things to be the way they once were.

I have seen thirty-year marriages base their existence and identity on the first two years of immature bliss, and man, them folks is *unhappy.*

You can't ever get back to the feeling of how things were when you first met. You did not know each other then.

It's retarded, it leaves no room for growth.

Lop, lop, lop the relationship back.

Allow it to be what it is, to nourish itself, and grow back again.

Teevee and the movies have, for many generations now, offered up false realities about what love is all about. Love stories evidently sell, and they end right when the couple comes together, gets married, and rides off into the sunset.

Happily-ever-afterness ensues. Wheeee!

The only problem with this is that most people don't cease to exist once they fall in love and get together with someone.

After that, your lives happen together.

And life is some butt-ugly shit sometimes. It's hard to be in love in the face of your or your lover's butt-ugly shit. That's where the real, true-blue, difficult love comes in. And yes, it's best to accept the fact of butt-ugly shit with someone who has your back, who really admires you, and who is committed to protecting your solitude. It isn't easy and it isn't fun, but it *is* love.

Once, I interviewed a brilliant performance artist named Kristen Kosmas. I asked her about love. She paraphrased Rainer Maria Rilke in *Letters to a Young Poet* and said, "The highest form of love is to protect another person's solitude."

I'd never read Rilke and looked for the quote Kristen referred to. I couldn't find it but found a similar one.

It goes like this:

"Love consists in this, that two solitudes protect and greet and touch each other."

I've always liked Kristen's version better. This is what she took away from Rilke, and it meant a lot to her. I heard what she heard, and it moved me as well.

I remember thinking about it while I was walking home after the interview. At the time, I was considering ending the relationship with boyfriend number two, and this quote really spurred me along.

I did not see him protecting my solitude.

I decided protecting solitude is what lover love was all about. A lover would know my deepest thoughts, traumas, and joys, as well as my body, sexuality, and how I express sexual intimacy. Someone who would know my family and all their truths. And mostly, someone who would know what an asshole I am, and proactively protect all of it.

Every last bit of me—not just the good things.

That's metaphorical solitude: all the things that make you, you. That which you can never escape from and that you will always face when you are alone with yourself.

When you can find someone who will protect that and when you are willing to protect that in someone else, dang. Sky's the limit with y'all.

Literal solitude is time. Everyone needs to have quiet time to reflect and be still with themselves.

Someone who actively protects my moments with myself? My god, I love you.

This deep love happens, and continues to happen, when you provide all the same services for your partner. And conversely, the ability to protect solitude only comes about through a lot of communication and spending time.

Also, people are failures.

Adam and Eve, Shakespeare, and Grimm's fairy tales are some of the stories that consistently remind us that humans fail.

We all have failings, no matter what. Sometimes they show up more often than usual. It's always *our* responsibility to have the courage to look at our failings, learn from them, and move on.

Nothing brings out our failings quite like sexual, romantic love.

No one is attractive, perfect, and great in every way. This never happens. Everyone is an ugly asshole in some way or another. The biggest trick to being in a committed sexual relationship with someone is to love what an asshole they are. This is tricky, I admit.

Misty Tenderlove is recalcitrant with her feelings. She tends to hold things in until she explodes. Sometimes she *tries* to communicate, and I totally think she is just telling me about the weather. She is from the South, and her communication style is rife with innuendo and codes that I find baffling and, frankly, fascinating. She might say, "I checked the oil in the car, and it seemed low." And I'm supposed to magically understand that she's communicating resentment over how much I ignore the car except for when I want to use it. It terrifies her to assert herself, but dang it, she tries, and I am constantly inspired by her courage.

I come from stock that hollers to raise the roof when we are unhappy. I have no problem saying something hurt my feelings or pissed me off. I am an emotional Abrams tank. I'll say, "What the fuck's up with the way you fold my pants? Stop folding my pants." Misty completely ignores this kind of communication and any attendant details. My style of communication strikes her as being unnecessarily rude and abrasive. I don't know if she's fascinated with it or not.

Probably not.

She has taught me the importance of pacing my words, and I have taught her the importance of saying "no" and "fuck off," but we will probably never improve greatly on either of these fronts. We struggle constantly with miscommunication. It is part of our marriage. My wife holds in her hurt and anger, and I jettison mine on the spot. This is an insurmountable gulf. Even if we go through three decades of therapy and counseling, she will still never jettison freely, and I will still never hold stuff in, and that's the way we are.

Jack Sprat could eat no fat.

I am who I am, and she is who she is.

And we love each other dearly.

Riz and Rob can't eat a meal at home together. I don't understand why exactly, but the only time they eat together is when they go out. That is how their relationship functions best.

Bob and Mako never go to bed angry with each other. This isn't because they have a pact, but because Mako loops all night long and won't leave Bob alone until they work things out.

Every relationship has problems, and sometimes they seem insurmountable. This is because they *are* insurmountable. These problems are allayed not by "fixing" them, but by accepting them.

And again, this does not mean someone gets a free pass to treat someone else like shit. Abusive behavior is never acceptable. Being an asshole is about human failings, not abuse.

Unconditionally loving the world doesn't mean being a pushover. Loving someone sometimes means drawing very clear boundaries and firmly asserting yourself. You do no one any favors by being a doormat. Saying "no" is sometimes the most honest and loving communication you can offer. Other folks may take comfort in manipulating or power tripping, but that is best left for them to face and deal with, should they choose to. And they will never choose to if no one ever says "no" to them. By making clear boundaries, you are loving yourself and providing someone with the opportunity to face themselves. Whether or not they seize the opportunity is none of your business.

Maybe you will inspire others, and maybe you will spark someone's imagination, but you will never, ever, ever, ever, ever, ever, ever, ever, ever change anyone.

There are repercussions for making boundaries. You can lose friendships, jobs, and even family relationships. It is difficult and sad to lose things and people that are important to you. But when you are firm about what you will and will not accept, you tend to attract other people and opportunities that will respect your boundaries without question.

Love is not a cakewalk in the park on a bright and sunny day, so forget about that.

The mainstream culture/environment will do *nothing* to assist you on any journey toward love. There are films and books that can offer support, but largely, only you can learn yourself some love.

The way to do this is to offer your love to the world, unconditionally.

This is almost impossible when someone jams their cart into the small of your back because they are *willing* the grocery-store line forward while texting their stockbroker, but it *can* be done.

As a culture, we meld sex and love with izzat in a very dysfunctional way, and the first folks to suffer from this are kids and teens. We grow up learning that if we're physically attractive to others, then we *must* be awesome. Our strength of character, intelligence, compassion, grace, sense of decency, loyalty, honesty, kindheartedness, and joviality do not matter, so long as we *look* good to others. Likewise, if we come to the understanding that we are not considered attractive, then all of our awesome qualities amount to jackshit. If we're fat, unathletic, poor, sickly, disabled, have bad hair or skin, then naturally, our "defects" will be pointed out to us on an almost daily basis.

Kids compete, bully, and belittle because that's what they see every livelong day in our violent environment.

I learned in my teen years that my worth as a human being was tied to my perceived sexual status through high school culture, friends, teevee, and movies. When I was a teenager, I had sex with people to bolster my self-esteem. It never worked, but my friends all did it, so I figured I'd be a pariah if I didn't do it too.

Nowadays, we have the whole "save it for marriage" trend going down. This is where girls pledge to their god, fathers, and future husbands (in that order) that they will save their virginity for their wedding night. I don't know what gay virgin girls are supposed to do, since our marriages are not legal, but there you have it.

If all this virginity business does such a great job of controlling teen sexuality, then why are the nation's highest teen pregnancy rates in the Bible Belt, Einstein?

Let's be clear, saving it for marriage *does not* mean *not having sex.* Teenagers with raging hormones cannot control the sexual force building inside of them.

Broadly defined, saving it for marriage means not having vaginal intercourse (this, by the way, is also Bill Clinton's definition of sex). This does not include oral sex, hand jobs, anal sex, and titty fucking. So now girls are learning—1950s June Cleaver–style—that sexual pleasure is mostly something for men and our job is to get pleasure out of his pleasure.

This is an acute retardation of progress.

The virginity trend is a cultural construct courtesy of the Victorian, puritan, and misogynist foundation and framework of our social environment.

Our concept of progress here is deeply mired in the past.

From my own experience as a young-timer, I believe in saving virginity—and all subsequent sex—for love and only love. Sex *never* happens between two people who don't care for each other deeply. Elaborate masturbation, procuring orgasm via the objectification of self and/or another, and projecting a perceived identity onto someone else happens—and none of that is sex.

Sexually protecting solitude is also big part of love.

As teenagers, we're pretty much left to the elements when it comes to sex and love. Sex education in schools—when it exists—is of absolutely no assistance. It merely teaches kids how babies are born and how to keep from getting diseases and procreating. What is lacking is an education about intimacy and mutual respect. *You don't have to have sexual intercourse with someone in order to experience sexual intimacy,* but boys want sex and girls want to feel loved, so teenage sex results from that.

A lot.

By the time young folks are in their late teens or early twenties, they've developed a very sophisticated language and belief system around sex. If you're not having sex, then something is "wrong" with you. You must have sex in order to "prove" to yourself and your peers that you are attractive and worthy of love. The more sex you have, the better. The more flippantly you discuss your sexual conquests, the more sophisticated you appear.

Reality teevee endlessly models canned versions of what passes for sexuality. This mostly involves adulterous heterosexuals, two girls going at it to somehow enrich their sexual attractiveness, the token homo and his/her (almost always his) conquests, or an endless series of one-night stands.

None of this is sex.

It is using someone else's body to bolster one's sense of self-worth and to achieve (or pretend to achieve) an orgasm.

Here is my definition of sex:

 ⊚   Biologically communing with another human being in the
     nakedness of your body and soul.

Get on down.

Here's my in-house computer definition of sex:

 ⊚   Same as sexual intercourse

 ⊚   Sexual behavior

This definition differential is why people almost universally feel
shitty about themselves after having a one-night stand. It's like
craving a home-cooked meal but eating a Bell Beefer.

All the stuff you see on teevee and the movies is not sex.

The porn industry is not sex.

Porn movies aren't even usually *about* sex.

Almost all porn is about power and control.

Power and control are the foundation of our nation.

Wheee.

Every time I have had sex with someone that I am not emotionally
invested in, I've felt bad. I allowed someone I did not know to
touch my solitude. Oh, lordisa, that's a bad feeling. It's definitely

possible to have sex with someone you are not in a serious relationship with, but it is imperative that you care for one another deeply.

Sex can only really happen between people who are emotionally invested in each other. Protecting someone's solitude in sex means knowing what comforts and pleases, knowing when to be gentle and knowing when it's hot to be beastly. You can only know these intimate realities when you spend time and invest yourself.

This can't happen overnight, it can't happen in two weeks, and it can't happen in six months. It takes a lot of time to know how to protect someone's solitude. A lot of time, a lot of love, investment, patience, curiosity, and caring.

One of the most powerful things two people can do together is learn how to have sex with each other. This can involve books, movies, music, and art, but mostly it's taking the time to talk and have sex. Like gender, sex is fluid. Maybe you've been married for twelve years, but the sex you and your partner need to be having now is not the same sex you were having when you first met. In fact, the time to learn about each other and to really start talking and exploring sexually is *after* the honeymoon phase, when the reality of someone's failings sets in.

Unfortunately, in our culture, we learn that when the going gets tough, it's time to find another lover.

The best way to be a great lover is to learn to listen. Listen to what your lover is saying, certainly, but moreover, listen to their body. A body will always tell you when something feels good, indifferent, bad. Listening to someone's body is a skill, and it cannot be learned if you don't also know how to listen to your own body.

Here are some of the ways your body talks to you:

It tells you when you need a rest. If you don't listen, it will get sick. It tells you when it needs nourishment and exercise. If you feed it bad food and do not exercise, your body will become out of shape and listless. If you continue to eat bad food and not exercise, you will probably become depressed, and if you *still* don't listen to your body, you could become obsessed with "fixing" your mind through (legal or illegal) drugs or alcohol. If you are uncomfortable or in a tense situation, your muscles might cramp up and complain. If you are in danger, your body will tell you before your mind does. It tenses, its hair raises, and the heartbeat quickens. Often, when someone is lying to you or otherwise mistreating you, your gut clenches up. Your body is talking to you all the time, and the more you listen to it, the more you will hear it saying stuff to you.

You can always, always, always trust your body. For people who have been abused, especially as children, this is a very hard lesson. It is nonetheless true.

In sex, you learn to trust someone with your body and you learn to honor the trust of someone else's body being in your hands.

When you're present in the world, sex has a meaning at odds with our frontier-nation-gone-wild definition.

The frontiersman dad does a pretty good job of controlling the biological function of human sexuality by forcing men to live up to freakish ideas of masculinity by giving them Viagra, by pitting women against each other for the sacrosanct prize of said man, and homos and queers who more or less emulate the larger culture's internecine gossip, lying, cheating, and stealing.

Still, he can't quite get sex out of the grasp of nature. Not like he's done with pooping and eating. Sexuality is a powerful force that must be tended to, just as one tends to one's izzat. People defy their own intelligence and experience and do really, deeply, incredibly stupid and/or violent things because of the power of sex and sexual love. Tiger Woods and John Edwards are good examples of people who suffer from the deep confusion that comes from the raw force of sexuality and deeply ingrained cultural constructs, allowing them to lie even to themselves.

I read this Dear Abby letter the other day, and it reminded me of what happens inside your heart when you get an idea of who you are, maybe realize the sacredness of your life, and shun any acquiescence with lies. This column featured letters responding to "The Other Woman," who evidently felt that life as a mistress was grand and that it wasn't her fault her lover's wife was a shrill bitch from hell. Or something to this effect. One woman wrote in, and this is what she said:

DEAR ABBY:

I was the other woman. Over time I have come to understand that I believed what I wanted to believe because I was lonely, needy and vulnerable. I learned as time went on that my lover was incapable of developing a mature, responsible and meaningful relationship. I experienced the calamitous consequences emotionally, psychologically and financially—as did our child.

Through counseling, friendships and networking with other women and getting to know myself in a rigorously honest way, I became too healthy to be the other woman. I'm now in the marriage I always dreamed of to a man with character and heart, who is devoted to me and "our" child. I learned that the right man would find me when I became the person he was looking for. It wasn't easy, but it was worth it.

—FINALLY FULFILLED

This is the sentence I love: "I became too healthy to be the other woman."

By engaging with those around her and getting to know herself in a "rigorously honest way," adultery just made no sense anymore.

She grew and found there was simply no place for the lies of passive violence in her life.

When you are intimately engaging with the world and those around you in a loving manner—and I don't mean folks you are emotionally invested in and are therefore assured of "getting something back" from them, I mean passersby, clerks, cashiers, wait staff, trash collectors, neighborhood critters, mail deliverers, crack heads on the corner, or kids who ask to mow the lawn—you are loving in a healthy way.

When you are fucking your best friend's husband, you are not.

If the rosebush is cut back and your marriage or relationship is suddenly a piece of shit and you are pining for the early days, you might seek to replicate this immature time by having affairs. A much more positive course of action would be to look at yourself, your fears and insecurities, your frustrations and weaknesses. No one else can help you out on this. If you ignore your own failings or refuse to accept your partner's, you will almost assuredly doom yourself to repeating the same immature honeymoon relationship over and over again.

Have fun with that.

When you are present in the world, sex is always a divine experience. And it can only happen with someone you trust deeply—someone who will not betray your nakedness by bragging to their friends about "bagging" you. Someone who does not live lies like being married to a person who is not you or insisting on being in the closet. You cannot open yourself up to someone you don't fully trust. And if you have sex with someone you don't fully trust, then you're not having sex (see above).

Sex moves through your body like a skeleton key, opening up all your fears and joys.

It's biology!

It is a nonvoluntary action like sneezing, breathing, and shitting!

In healthy sexual relationships, you share yourself with someone else—your secrets, traumas, hopes, and dreams. What moves you to orgasm, what moves you past one into three more. And you take in, respect, and bear witness to your lover's pain, sexuality, memories, imagination, and pleasure.

The only other time I've experienced that same kind of deep biology-based intimacy is with my family. Not in a creepy, incestuous way. I mean my siblings, parents and me knew biological and intimate things about each other that no one else really knew. Nick had to shit the moment he was halfway home from school. He did not like to poop at school, and it was a daily laugh to see him holding his ass as he tore through the front door. We knew when our mom was on her period, when our dad would hog the bathroom reading the *Los Angeles Times*, and when someone was (hilariously, unless it was you) going through puberty.

In a sexual context, these are all the same kinds of things you know about your lover. Pussy farts, premature ejaculation, not being able to achieve orgasm, and not being able to keep a woody are some of the sexual intimacies lovers share. These biological realities often bring up feelings of shame or embarrassment because of our disconnect from nature.

People think sex is voluntary, but people are wrong. If you don't have good, honest, healthy sex and love (just like you hopefully have good, honest, healthy poops twice a day), all that pent up sexual force inside of you will come out in other ways.

Sometimes people can get sex out of their body by positive and beneficial means, like through art or music, perhaps.

Sometimes people with pent up sexual energy become objectum sexuals, who fall in love with—and often marry—objects, such as the Berlin Wall, a railing in a train station, or a broken down carnival ride.

Sometimes, actually quite often, you get yer rapists and killers.

A lot of that communist sharing goes down in healthy sex and love.

People who don't learn to share generally develop few compassion skills, and sociopathic tendencies from childhood and adolescence become much more complex and acute in adulthood.

When people don't experience and respect that deep kind of biological sharing, a potentially damaging isolation sets in.

Dylan Klebold, Eric Harris, Seung-Hui Cho, Michael Devlin, Phillip Garrido, Timothy McVeigh, thousands of Catholic priests, Andrea Yates, the BTK killer, and many other violent criminals all experience(d) varying forms and degrees of biological isolation.

Still, there are some aspects of isolation that can be profoundly life changing. Great epiphanies and ideas come from failure and feelings of hopelessness or depression. Grief, trauma, and anger fuel some of the most powerful political movements, art, and music the world has ever known. There is great potential in the hard times of isolation. I have found the trick of isolation is if I just keep muddling through it, eventually, it will be over and I will have awesome new insights, friends, passions, interests, or plans. The problem is, you don't know how long the hard time will last and there is no light for you while you are muddling through the darkness of your despair.

The youngest kid in our family, Nick, lost his (our) life in a car accident when he was sixteen years old. I was going to school in Olympia at Evergreen. My mother told me on the phone, and I have hated answering the phone ever since.

Our Grammy oversaw the planting of the rosebushes for our mom. She and others who knew Nick and shared our grief understood that this was gonna be a long haul.

It was.

I went back to Olympia, and things got bad, fast. Few knew of my grief, and those who did had no idea how seriously awesome Nick was. He was the nicest, funniest kid in our family. He got along with everyone, and no one really got along with anyone else all the time. I missed him so badly over time. The enormity of him being gone just got worse and worse, and counterproductively, the more time passed, the more people figured I should probably be "over it." I had no place to grieve and no one to grieve with, so I tried to express my feelings in my writing and schoolwork, but the grief was too big and I was too small.

Eventually the grief boiled over into the world, and I started to cut myself with pieces of broken glass and burn myself with incense. The idea was that if I could see that the physical healing process was going on in different stages at all times, then I *must* be experiencing emotional healing as well. I hid the wounds well and kept three to five in varying stages of healing for a year or so.

Along with writing, this is how I moved through the worst of my grief and was able to get it out of my body before doing something irretrievably stupid. Wounding myself was what I came up with on the fly and is also another one of those darling paradoxes where physical violence sustained my life.

This was a choice I made when a very bad feeling breathed each breath with me. In that pristine viewing mechanism called retrospect, I can think of ten other nonviolent choices. Keeping in mind that it was almost physically impossible to engage with anyone who did not know my brother, and that my budget was very low, I still could have:

1. Apprenticed at an organic farm in the area.
2. Rustled up two turntables and a microphone.
3. Built a gigantic bird or tree house, using found detritus.
4. Planted a garden.
5. Learned how to make fancy cakes.
6. Entered a dance-off.
7. Trained for an eighteen-mile run.
8. Gathered and delivered food to old people and homeless shelters.
9. Recontextualized ads on billboards.
10. Found presents for strangers and nestled them in trees or other places.

When your heart's broken, though, it's not easy coming up with good ideas, but I did manage to find a way to heal while living in an environment/culture that offered me none, and now that I have had that experience, I have better responses and am stronger and more resilient when isolation shows up again from time to time.

And, I learned about the strange gifts that grief and isolation bring.

My father had an audio- and photographic memory. Soon after he died, I started remembering numbers. I know credit- and library-card numbers and the phone numbers of everyone I call with any frequency.

After my Grammy died, the sudden ability and desire to bake hit me like a bolt of lightning. I can now make gorgeous tiered cakes that feed two hundred people.

When Nick died, I inherited his love and compassion and became much more engaged with the world around me. Nick's love was a fundamental love, a rare love, a love that didn't ask a lot of questions and included everyone. And so, this book is an homage to the gift my brother willed to me.

If the humans were at odds, if there was tension and anger in the house, ol' Nick took his big-ass love outside and hung out with Methadream, our desert tortoise, or the chickens, the cats, the dog.

Whoever.

He made ecosystems, freeways, Saran-Wrap lined fountains, loving the earth, loving the mud. He loved me, JoeB, Liz, Mom, and Dad. He had positive and intimate relationships with all of us, no matter who was being an asshole to whom.

That is how Nick rolled.

And when Nick died, I started rolling like that too.

Me n' my boyfriend went out into the forest after my mom told us about the car accident. We built a shrine out there, and I kneeled down and begged the world not to take him.

But instead, I felt a churning wave of his big-ass love crash into my heart, and I knew he was gone and I wailed.

That is when I found out that just like there are external bombs, like the one in Hiroshima, there are also internal bombs that do the same thing, only you usually keep living and no one else can really see the damage.

But Nick's love stayed there in my heart and it grew.

Before Nick died, for instance, I was terrified of dogs.

Until I reached my midtwenties, if I saw a dog coming toward me—on or off a leash, it didn't matter—I'd cross the street. Sometimes take a different route altogether. This fear traces back to getting attacked by a neighbor's dog as a child when I jumped their fence to get our ball, and that terror kept a firm grasp on my consciousness.

It grew as I grew, and by the time I was in my midtwenties, it had a firmly established place in my heart.

But with Nick's gift inside of me, I could no longer maintain this fear. His big-ass love hogged up all the room in my heart, and it was just too crowded, you know? A lot of things had to go and being afraid of dogs was one of them.

So I started small.

If I saw an obviously happy dog firmly leashed outside a café with large windows so people might come to my aid if it suddenly tried to tear my face off, I would force myself to pet the dog.

I made a rule that I must pet every dog I saw in this context, no matter where I was going or when I was supposed to be there.

When I got okay with that, the rules expanded *a smidge.*

I would pet dogs in front of grocery stores, where people might not be able to come to my rescue.

Then I'd pet small dogs stopped at street corners with their persons.

On and on this progressed, every week or so—wee triumphs.

It took me two or three years to get to where I'd seriously romp with and love up dogs just like Nick always did.

I am no longer afraid of dogs at all.

I love dogs; they are the best of friends.

The person I was before Nick died is much different from the one after. I was pretty much like every other self-absorbed, vaguely dissatisfied, politically enraged person taking up space on the planet. I doubt I would have ever written a book if Nick did not die and will his love to me.

If I could swap book-writin' for Nick, oh hot damn, I'd do it in a New York minute.

If I could swap being a big-hearted person for Nick to be alive again, I wouldn't hesitate.

But this can never happen, so I try to make the most of his gift. I have grown accustomed to Nick's love being a part of me for two decades, and it's taken on a life of its own.

Before Nick died, I thought love was all about two people having fabulous sex with each other all the time, going on fun trips together, and being lovers. Maybe settling down one day, getting hitched, having kids.

Sex is a good thing and having a lover is a good thing, but it is no more life changing than enacting love toward every being I come into contact with.

Here are some ways to love:

a) being present

b) interacting with the organic world surrounding your organic body

c) touching an organic substance

d) listening to the wind

e) smelling the air

f) picking oranges off the neighbor's tree

g) playing with the kids, dogs, chickens, and goats

h) being aware that the full moon is fabulously glowing in the sky

i) intimately engaging with a loved one who is physically present and thereby communicating realities, fears, hopes, desires, needs, and possible resentments that require your physical energy and emotional attention

j) baking sweets for birthdays

k) building a chicken coop

l) raising chickens and bartering great stuff for fresh eggs

m) knitting a tea cozy

n) dancing, which, second only to sex, is *the most important* physical/emotional activity you can practice

o) disciplining the kids, dogs, chickens, and goats

p) planting seeds

q)   tending to the seedlings
r)   tending to the plants
s)   harvesting your bounty
t)   volunteering
u)   jerry rigging a tree fort
v)   gathering up trash somewhere trashy
w)   helping the lady struggling to get on the bus with groceries, her toddler, and baby in the stroller
x)   using your voice to communicate
y)   having healthy confrontations
z)   cleaning house

With or without you, love exists in the world. Just like violence, just like war. The most awesome, most fun challenge is bringing all this love out into the violent world we live in. Consciously choosing to be a life force inside of love's ecosystem is a way to actually thrive. It requires imagination, a sense of humor, creativity, resourcefulness, openheartedness, and figuring out how to make the very, very best out of the very, very worst. With all the pain and grief that love brings, it is nevertheless very, very fun to enact love in our daily lives.

This is how we can reconnect with nature and our own humanity. This is how we can protect ourselves and the world we live in.

After I was bequeathed Nick's love and after Arun Gandhi's words sent me on a knowledge quest, I started doing this thing where I would conjure up the love I have for my sister and then I would pretend that I had this exact same love for everyone I came into contact with. Like in the grocery store, as I was handing the cashier my money, I'd look at her and think about the love Liz and I have, and she would just erupt into this huge smile. Or I'd do it when I thanked my mailman or held a door open for a grandmother with a stroller and a toddler. Every time I did this, I'd feel this warm gush of love flowing all over the place.

Sometimes I have problems with my sister and she pisses me off, or she has problems with me and I piss her off. But I held her in my arms on the way home from the hospital after she was born, and no matter how much she sucks and no matter how much I suck, we are still sisters and we love each other heartily. I chose that familiar, comfortable love as the one to direct toward people.

Sometimes people suck, but regardless, I make myself pretend that I have that same love for them.

This doesn't mean I'm a namby-pamby who doesn't speak my mind, act out in anger, or is generally an asshole. I *am* a total asshole. I just force myself to look at how much love there really is in my heart and consciously allow it a place in my life and in the world.

It became a kind of habit to interact with people from that strong place of love.

Over time, I found that I became a happier person.

I know this sounds very corny, but that is only because it is a cultural construct to look upon one another with distrust or solely within the limited scope of our self-interests.

Those things are reflections of the society we were born into and not necessarily reflections of us as family members, friends, lovers, or total strangers.

You might notice an absence of tension when you engage with someone you do not know in a spirit of familiar and comfortable love. You might even notice an alien warmth or closeness. That feeling—however fleeting—is a result of loving the world.

So these things happened, where I had more love in my heart and became happier. I found that my happiness brings out happiness in others. In doing this, many learned behaviors came to the surface of my consciousness, and I saw the patent absurdity therein.

I realized that I *am* my thoughts and actions.

And this reminded me of another thing I have heard all my life, something I have believed since I learned about a chicken's journey into my red and white bucket: You are what you eat.

This is the thing.

Having faith in god—whatever you perceive god to be—may or may not serve you, I don't know. Having faith in love, however, will always serve you, in every imaginable capacity. Learning how to seek out and protect love is a skill, and as I have mentioned, our culture/environment will do little to shore things up for you. Strip away your indoctrination, and you will see the love that surrounds you.

Every day, I pray.

Sometimes I do this while I feed the birds and other critters in the neighborhood. It takes about ten minutes to tear up half a loaf of day-old bread. During that time, I am quiet and thinking about the animals.

I wish them the very, very best.

This is a prayer.

I give thanks for the people and animals around me. I give thanks for the people and animals that are not around me. I offer what I can and give thanks. This generates an enormous amount of love.

It is very simple and powerful.

How can you love the world?

Let you count the ways.

Acknowledgments

As always, thanks to my mom because you are a shining light. So many things I would not see without the light of you, Mom. I love you. Thanks.

Misty, thanks for doing more shit around the house so I can write. That's very kind of you. Thanks for being patient when I am distracted and preoccupied. Thanks for loving me for who I am and not wanting me to be the person you think I am.

Bob and Mako, thanks for the onigiri, nabemono, laughter, great ideas, and gentle pounding. Thanks for the book cover, your love, support, and for spending time.

Thanks to everyone else in my family: Liz, JoeB, Josh, Cindy, Avery, Evan, Joseph, and Nicholas. Your love means the world to me.

Crystal, I was such a mess when you asked me to write this book. I don't know if I would have ever written another book if it wasn't for you. Thanks for encouraging me and making sense of my jumbledy-jumble. I can't underscore this enough: there would be no *Rose* without your grace and tenacity. I should really thank you first, but all those other folks would get bent out of shape about it.

Thanks to everyone else at Seven Stories too. It's a hard go making it as an independent press, and y'all work yer asses off and do a stellar job. Maybe that's where Crystal gets her tenacity.

Thanks to the warriors Deb, Eli, Jen, Maricela, and Tina. Your thoughts and experiences resonated inside me throughout the years of working on this book and beyond. You inspire, ignite, and delight. Thank you.

Susan, Lilyhammer, and Anna, thanks for your friendship and all the happy times.

Thanks to everyone at the refugee office: Greg, Sumonnat, Margo, Erica, Daniel, Mag, Nada, Khamson, Hong, Kevin, Kyle, Lucas, and Warren. Special thanks to Erica for giving me a chance, Margo for your general loveliness and compelling conversation, and to Sumonnat for not firing me for being distracted and preoccupied.

Thanks to Blanca and Mahatma for filling in the cuddly/cranky niche.

Riz and Rob, same thing. It's a big niche.

Goats and chickens, thanks to you as well. Best friends ever when the chips are up or down.

And Cedric, always Cedric. There're always thanks in the world for Cedric, and I have some of them.

Also, as usual, my thanks to Stan Goff and Steven E. Flusty, for being shining and beautiful.

Thanks to Esther and Eddie for a lifelong friendship and many happy river times.

Thanks to Spanky, Jon, Lolo, and Grover for your love, kindness, and for hooking us up with the best home ever. Thanks to Greg for coming over with Spanky and fixing stuff and grumbling at each other like a married couple and making us laugh our asses off. Plus, you are both great at fixing stuff. Thanks to Lori just because you rock.

Iman, Ali, Zahara, Ammar, Ghaith, and Anmar, thanks for coming to the US. Thanks for gracing our lives with your warmth and kindheartedness. Thanks for teaching us about Islam and for feeding us the best food ever.

Margaret and Cyrus, thanks for the food and the love and the general circle of coolness.

Since I seem to thank everybody for food, I guess I'd be amiss if I didn't thank food. Thanks, food. You're the best.

Many thanks to all the schools and conferences that have invited me to come and speak. It is not only a great honor, but also allows me time to do things like work on a book. Special thanks to the Women's Center at the University of California, San Diego, for going up against the racism on campus. You ladies rock.

Lastly, thanks to Colton Harris-Moore for giving me a hearty, years-long, perpetual chuckle that I've enjoyed throughout the writing of this book. It's a bummer you got caught, but I'm thankful you weren't killed.

INGA MUSCIO is the author of *Cunt: A Declaration of Independence* and *Autobiography of a Blue-Eyed Devil*. She lives in the Pacific Northwest and lectures widely across the nation. For more information, visit www.ingalagringa.com.

SEVEN STORIES PRESS is an independent book publisher based in New York City, with distribution throughout the United States, Canada, England, and Australia. We publish works of the imagination by such writers as Nelson Algren, Russell Banks, Octavia E. Butler, Ani DiFranco, Assia Djebar, Ariel Dorfman, Coco Fusco, Barry Gifford, Hwang Sok-yong, Peter Plate, Lee Stringer, and Kurt Vonnegut, to name a few, together with political titles by voices of conscience, including the Boston Women's Health Collective, Noam Chomsky, Angela Y. Davis, Human Rights Watch, Derrick Jensen, Ralph Nader, Loretta Napoleoni, Gary Null, Project Censored, Ted Rall, Barbara Seaman, Alice Walker, Gary Webb, and Howard Zinn, among many others. Seven Stories Press believes publishers have a special responsibility to defend free speech and human rights, and to celebrate the gifts of the human imagination, wherever we can. For additional information, visit www.sevenstories.com.